THE KINGDOM OF GOD IS ANARCHY

THE KINGDOM OF GOD IS ANARCHY

Christian Nonviolence and Negative Political Theology

JOHANNES AAKJÆR STEENBUCH

CASCADE *Books* • Eugene, Oregon

THE KINGDOM OF GOD IS ANARCHY
Christian Nonviolence and Negative Political Theology

Cascade Books
An Imprint of Wipf and Stock Publishers
199 W. 8th Ave., Suite 3
Eugene, OR 97401

www.wipfandstock.com

PAPERBACK ISBN: 979-8-3852-4395-2
HARDCOVER ISBN: 979-8-3852-4396-9
EBOOK ISBN: 979-8-3852-4397-6

Cataloguing-in-Publication data:

Names: Steenbuch, Johannes Aakjær, author.

Title: The kingdom of God is anarchy : Christian nonviolence and negative political theology / Johannes Aakjær Steenbuch.

Description: Eugene, OR: Cascade Books, 2026 | Includes bibliographical references.

Identifiers: ISBN 979-8-3852-4395-2 (paperback) | ISBN 979-8-3852-4396-9 (hardcover) | ISBN 979-8-3852-4397-6 (ebook)

Subjects: LCSH: Christianity and politics. | Anarchism. | Christian anarchism.

Classification: BS672 S65 2026 (paperback) | BS672 (ebook)
VERSION NUMBER 03/12/26

The religious truth of anarchism consists in this, that power over humanity is bound up with sin and evil, that a state of perfection is a state where there is no power of human over human, that is to say, anarchy. The kingdom of God is freedom and the absence of such power; no categories of the exercise of such power are to be transferred to it. The kingdom of God is anarchy.

—NICOLAI BERDYAEV (1874–1948)

Contents

Preface

THIS book is an essay based on a longer work published in Danish in 2019. The title of that book was *Guds rige er anarki*, which translates as *The Kingdom of God Is Anarchy*—a claim originally made by the Russian philosopher Nicolai Berdyaev about how (only) the kingdom of God is free from power and domination. In the book I used this claim as an offset for a more or less systematic exploration of how the kingdom of God offers an alternative to human claims to power and domination. Drawing on studies of early Christian theology and contemporary theological critiques of authority, power, and domination, I attempted to flesh out some of the implications of the idea of the kingdom of God as "anarchy." What follows is an abbreviated and more essayistic version of some of my reflections in English.

In the following, "anarchy" is, of course, not understood in the negative sense of chaos and arbitrary violence but quite the opposite: By anarchy, I mean a certain kind of order that is not based on authoritarian rule, violence, domination, and power, but on egalitarian freedom and love. It is this kind of anarchy that characterizes the kingdom of God. It is also, it will be argued, this kind of anarchy that should characterize the Christian church in its preaching and practice.

I have not made use of contemporary perspectives from, for example, gender and race studies, or critical theory, as I do not find myself in a position of having much of value to say on these issues.

Instead, I have confined myself to saying something about those parts of the theological tradition that I know to be relevant to the topic of "Christian anarchism." These are especially "classical" patristic sources on the one hand, and a modern one with roots in twentieth-century dialectical theology on the other. This may seem an odd combination (although Neo-Orthodoxy *is* a thing!). The following is simply a sketch of how these traditions might be applied to each other.

The intention is not to persuade anyone to identify as a "Christian anarchist" or even to contribute to this or that movement, whether political or ecclesial. The purpose is simply to explore some aspects of the gospel narrative from this peculiar perspective. Hopefully some insights will be gained that may prove useful or just meaningful in whatever context we might find ourselves. In a time of increasing authoritarian attitudes towards politics and religion globally—the examples are too numerous to mention—this approach to theology, church, and politics may prove quite relevant.

This short book is not a "scholarly" work, although I do draw on ideas that I have picked up during my work with historical theology, especially early Christian studies ("patristics"). This is why I have in most cases only provided precise footnotes and bibliographical information to historical works. A selection of literature is provided in the bibliography. I realize that my documentation may seem a bit arbitrary, but I've simply included the works that I found most relevant for further studies on the topic. I have used a variety of Bible translations as I thought appropriate, but primarily the New International Version.

—Johannes Steenbuch, Nylars 2025

Introduction

Christian Anarchism?

"The time has come," he said. "The kingdom of God has come near. Repent and believe the good news!"

—MARK 1:15

THESE words of Jesus according to the Gospel of Mark constitute the fundamentals of the good news, the gospel. Jesus, who is himself the subject matter of Christianity, proclaimed the immanence of the kingdom of God, and called people to faith and repentance—not as a threat, but because the message of the kingdom was good news for "all the people" (Luke 2:10). The gospel is about the presence of the kingdom of God.

But what is the "kingdom of God"? The Russian philosopher and theologian Nicolai Berdyaev (1874–1948) argued that "the kingdom of God is anarchy."[1] By this he meant that the kingdom of God is a state of affairs without relations of power and domination among humans. While critical of anarchism as a political movement—he saw it as naive and destructive because of its materialistic underpinnings—Berdyaev acknowledged the "religious truth" of anarchism. The self-government of human beings means a concord between inner and outer freedom. The kingdom of God consists of a kind of freedom that makes all power and domination

1. Berdyaev, *Slavery and Freedom*, 148.

obsolete. That this state of affairs is immanent in the work of Jesus Christ is the good news, the gospel.

"No God, no master!" was a favorite slogan of modern political anarchism (Blanqui). The idea was that the concept of God must be abolished since religion has historically been used to legitimize oppression. This makes sense if "God" means a principle that sits at the top of a hierarchy of power. This is not, however, the Christian concept of God. In classical Christian theology as it was developed especially in the fourth century, God as creator was conceived of as radically different from everything in this world (what Sokolowski has called "the Christian distinction"), and therefore not as part of a hierarchical order. Every created being is equally distant from God and, as such, of equal value, said the important Cappadocian theologian Gregory of Nyssa (c. 335–395).[2] In the words of the twentieth-century Swiss theologian Karl Barth in his commentary on Romans, the power of God is not the most exalted of all observable forces, but the *crisis* of all power.

While the term "anarchy" in the secular, political vocabulary means "without leader or ruler," it may also hold a theological significance. The term essentially means without beginning or principle, *archê*. Since the first centuries Christian theologians have described God as *anarchos*—a great Greek-Byzantine Christmas hymn still in use is called *Anarchos Theos*. Although in classical Trinitarian theology, often only God the Father was said to be *anarchos*, in the strict sense, the Son was said to be eternally begotten from the Father with an "anarchic" birth. There is, for this reason, no order of submission and domination in the Trinity, but the Son fully shares in the kingdom of God.

In fact, as theologians have sometimes argued, Jesus is himself the kingdom, the *auto-basileia* or the kingdom-in-itself (Origen, Barth).[3] The kingdom of God is not something separate from Jesus, but is present wherever he is present. To participate in

2. Gregory of Nyssa, *Catechetical Discourse* 27, 4. The heavenly powers, angels, etc., are as far away from God as we are, since God is infinite. See also Gregory of Nazianzus, *Oration* 28, 3.

3. Origen, *Commentary on Matthew* 14, 7; 10, 7.

the kingdom of God is to participate in the life of Christ, to "be" in Christ, as Paul described it (2 Cor 5:17). The gospel is about a kingdom that is anarchy in the sense of not being founded upon an original act of violence or subjugation. As David Bentley Hart once wrote, the new world brought into being in the Gospels is a positively "anarchic" order that casts everything in a new light. Participating in the kingdom of God means participating in God's love and freedom through Christ.

In what follows, I will use the term "anarchy" in the specifically modern sense of freedom from domination and hierarchy. To this degree, the claim that "the kingdom of God is anarchy" can be seen as a matter of so-called "political theology." Political theology is traditionally understood as an attempt to understand, ground, or legitimize a political order in theological terms. However, if the notion of the kingdom of God as anarchy fits this description, it does not do so neatly. It is perhaps rather what has sometimes been described as a "negative political theology." The gospel of the kingdom is not exactly "political," since it cannot be used to legitimize any political order—but it is not exactly "apolitical" either, since it is critical to how we conceive human relations. In a sense, it transcends the political/apolitical distinction by negating both. As author Mark van Steenwyk has put it, the kingdom of God is an "unkingdom" of which Jesus is the "unking." Transcending both the political and the apolitical alike, the presence of the kingdom transforms both the (supposedly) political and apolitical spheres of human life.

From the idea of the kingdom of God as anarchy follows a practice that can perhaps be called "Christian anarchism." Anarchism in general can be understood as a tendency to criticize all illegitimate power structures (Chomsky), rather than a political "ideology." Anarchism is the rejection of any attempt to mediate human relations through external "representation." Representation is abstraction—the opposite of the concrete, direct relationship between people. In positive terms, anarchism may, as such, be understood as practices that seek alternatives to abstract power through grassroots work. While a "Christian anarchism" should be founded on theological principles, it will often display a similar attitude in how we conceive Christian ethics, the role and form of the church, and so on.

The links between Christian theology and practice on the one hand, and a radical, anti-authoritarian rejection of all forms of domination on the other, are far from new. The German philosopher and famous atheist Friedrich Nietzsche (1844–1900) described the early Christians as "holy anarchists," who subverted the Roman Empire with their insistence on humility and pacifism. Nietzsche even complained that there is "a perfect likeness between the Christian and the anarchist."[4] Their "object and instinct," he argued, "point only to destruction." Nietzsche, who saw the unfettered "will to power" as the highest virtue, was highly critical of Christianity's "slave morality." However, his identification of the Christian *ethos* with a kind of anarchist rejection of power and authority cannot be easily dismissed.

Throughout church history, Christian thinkers have frequently returned to Jesus' original critique of political and religious oppression, emphasizing his proclamation of the kingdom of God in which power is replaced by love, and authority by freedom. The apostle Paul—even if his thinking is at times regarded as somewhat authoritarian—made it clear that Jesus will eventually destroy "all dominion, authority and power" (1 Cor 15:24), and that Christians are enrolled in a spiritual battle against the authorities and powers of "this dark world" (Eph 6:12). For Christians, this fight meant not engaging in any kind of violence or domination. The best way to fight power was to not engage in power.

Early Christians were ambivalent in their attitude toward secular authorities. On the one hand, the emperor's office was often seen as divinely ordained. On the other hand, early Christians frequently identified the Roman Empire with the beast in Daniel's apocalypse and the "city on seven hills" in the apocalypse of John. They refused to participate in the imperial cult and to serve as soldiers. Tatian (c. 110–180) wrote: "I do not wish to be a ruler, I have

4. Nietzsche, *Antichrist*, 58.

no interest in being rich, I reject military service."[5] To follow Jesus meant to imitate his rejection of power and wealth. "Happiness," argued the unknown author of the *Epistle to Diognetus* from the second century, is *not* "to oppress one's neighbor, to want more than the weak, to be rich, or to use violence against the oppressed," adding that it is not possible to imitate God through violence and domination, since these things are "foreign to God."[6] When the pagan philosopher Celsus complained that Christians did not partake in militarily defending society against barbarians, the influential theologian Origen (c. 185–253) replied that Christians had a different job to do—works of love and prayer.[7]

The Christian rejection of pagan religion was seen as detrimental to society, which seems to have been a major reason why it was fatal to identify as a Christian. Christians were persecuted and killed, some were thrown to the lions and some were burned alive. The early Christians were not persecuted for proclaiming that you could go to heaven when you died, but for confessing that "Jesus is Lord" in a society where Caesar claimed to be lord (Zahnd). When Christians refused to honor the emperor as a god, they were, in the eyes of the authorities, complicit in breaking down the social order. Christians were accused of being atheists—which was arguably more or less the same as calling them "anarchists."

All this gradually changed, of course. In the fourth century—when Christianity had gained ground in the Roman Empire despite persecution—the church went from being a persecuted minority to being a close ally of the powers. From being an illegal religion, Christianity went to becoming the only religion legal in 380 AD. This did not mean, however, that there was no longer any Christian criticism of power. On the contrary. The "Christianization" of society even made it possible to criticize power in new ways: When people claimed to be Christians, it now made sense to blame people for not living according to their professed beliefs.

5. Tatian, *Address to the Greeks* 11,2.

6. *Epistle to Diognetus* 10,5.

7. Origen, *Against Celsus* 8, 73.

In any case, we see quite a few examples of how power is criticized from the fourth century and onward.

In the Middle Ages, radical movements appeared—such as the Lollards—that in different measures criticized the alliance between church and state, often rejecting violence, authority, and property on principle. In the sixteenth century, a theological critique of power appeared in the radical wing of the Reformation, and again with the Diggers in seventeenth-century England and parts of Radical Pietism on the Continent in the eighteenth century. More recently there have been explicit examples of Christian anarchism. In the American context the perhaps best known example is Dorothy Day (1897–1980) and her Catholic Worker movement. In the European context should be mentioned the French lawyer and Reformed theologian Jacques Ellul (1912–1994), whose small book with the English title *Anarchy and Christianity* has gained the status of a neo-classic.

Today, drawing on these traditions, a wide variety of theologians, churches, and laypeople are active in working out an "anarchist" way of being church. The roots of these traditions can in many cases be traced to early twentieth-century radicals like Christoph Blumhardt (1842–1919), who saw the gospel as a message about the kingdom of God that is breaking in on the world. Such "Christian anarchism" typically perceives the kingdom of God as radically opposed to any conceivable secular political order. Vernard Eller explained that Christian anarchy is fundamentally "dialectical." The resurrection is a revolution that radically disrupts all worldly order (Barth). This is why the kingdom of God cannot be identified with any existing political order, but must always be seen as the negation of the status quo—as well as all attempts at overthrowing society through violent means.

Of course, while the gospel is revolutionary in its own way, "Christian anarchism" will have to differ from secular forms of anarchism that often see violence as a legitimate tool in the struggle against power. Christian anarchists are typically pacifist, seeing nonviolence, civil disobedience, and grassroots work as the only true Christian alternatives to power and violence, be it reactionary or revolutionary in kind. Jacques Ellul, for example, defined Christian anarchism as the total rejection of violence in all its forms. This perspective is much needed in the light of current conflicts. The polarization that characterizes much of the political landscape globally today calls for new perspectives on religion and politics. To meet contemporary challenges, the church cannot take its cues from secular ideologies, not even "anarchism." It is necessary once again to reach back to the theological roots.

As already mentioned, classical Trinitarian theology insisted on the unity and equal value of the Father, Son, and Holy Spirit. This, it was sometimes argued, should be reflected in human relations. All humans are by nature of equal value, said Gregory of Nyssa in his argument against theological subordinationism.[8] This is why, he noted, humans have an instinctive tendency to make themselves equal to their superiors by rebelling against power. Since humanity is one, it is absurd to divide people up into "masters" and "slaves," Gregory noted in his famous critique of slavery.[9] All people are equally created in the image of God, and should as such participate in God's freedom. "Liberty," argued Gregory's sister Macrina the Younger (c. 324–379), means coming up to a "self-regulating" state with "no master."[10] In other words: "One triune God, no master," to rewrite the anarchist slogan quoted above. Or, as another slogan puts it, "If God is master, then man must be slave" (Bakunin), but for the early Christians it was precisely by participating in God's freedom that humans could be free.

Today, postmodern strains of political philosophy and theology tend to privilege the "other" and "difference" over the "identical" and "sameness." The classical notion of participation is viewed as problematic as it—presumably—violates the individual and particular. As an apparent subspecies of "monotheism," Christianity is

8. Gregory of Nyssa, *Against Eunomius* 1,1,527– 528.

9. Gregory of Nyssa, *Sermon on Ecclesiastes* 336.

10. Macrina according to Gregory of Nyssa, *On the Soul and the Resurrection* 103. Macrina was not making a "political" point, but one about self-control over our passions. However, her notion of freedom clearly plays a role in Gregory's critique of power and domination in human relations.

often met with suspicion by radicals and liberals alike, who seek ways of thinking that allow for plurality rather than totalitarian uniformity. Yet, as Athanasius (c. 296–373) argued, it is precisely because the world was created by God that there can be differences in the world, rather than a monotonous homogeneity.[11] Christian theology, moreover, speaks of the incarnation of God. God is not just a distant reality, indifferent to or hovering above the world, but the kingdom of God has become immanent in the concrete person of Christ in a way that bypasses all abstract political power.

Participation in the anarchic love and freedom of Christ does not mean violently suppressing everything particular or different in order to conform to some idea of divine unity. God's oneness does not mean singularity, argued Gregory of Nyssa, but a community of persons.[12] The kingdom of God, it seems, embraces an infinity of differences that nevertheless come together in a harmonious whole. With the Trinitarian view of God, early Christian theology had already overcome the dichotomy between unity and plurality, the "one" and the "many." It did so by seeing the world as created by a God who consists of the loving unity of different but equal persons. This love—"God is love" (1 John 4:8)—is the governing principle in the kingdom of God. As such the kingdom of God is antithetical to all forms of authoritarian and totalitarian politics. At the same time, however, it avoids the dissolution that results from contemporary postmodern, nihilistic worldviews.

Such perspectives, informed by Trinitarian theology, are relevant to how the church perceives current issues in culture and politics. In this, "Christian anarchism" can have a peculiar voice, if only as a reminder that the kingdom of God is radically different from the kingdoms—political orders of any kind—of this world. It is a reminder that another world is possible, as they say. In what follows, we will take a closer look at how all this plays out in the biblical narrative—and how it can be perceived theologically.

11. Athanasius, *On the Incarnation* 2.

12. Gregory of Nyssa, *Against Eunomius* 3, 20–21.

I.

From Paradise to Politics

God saw all that he had made, and it was very good.

—GENESIS 1:31

COMMENTATORS have often noted how the biblical account of the creation in Genesis differs from other myths of creation. God does not create by force or violence, or by first overcoming evil in order to make something good. God simply speaks and by the Word, the divine *logos*, creates the world *ex nihilo,* out of nothing. When God in the Christian tradition is called "pantocrator," the ruler of all, Origen argued that this means that God maintains and provides for all things through the Son, the divine *logos*, who rules by wisdom rather than by force and necessity.[1] If the Greek word *logos* can also be translated as "narrative," then creation is literally the good story gently told by God. Evil and violence enter the world only as humanity turns away from God. This happens when humanity attempts to become like God by eating from the "tree of the knowledge of good and evil" (Gen 3:1–7).

Now, of course, much have been said about the meaning of "the fall." Early theologians like Irenaeus and Athanasius argued with Paul that death is a common reality because we have collectively turned our backs on the source of life. Perhaps most relevant

1. Origen, *On First Principles* 1, 2, 10.

to our purpose, it is worth noting, however, that in Genesis, sin is essentially described as humanity's attempt at becoming "like God" by acquiring the capacity for moral judgment. Initially, humans are meant to live in spontaneous love and trust in God and one another, but as morality is introduced, spontaneity is replaced by an objectified, judgmental attitude. In other words, the story of the fall portrays how sin is fundamentally humanity's attempt to become gods by ruling over themselves and each other. The result is violence and domination, which is how death comes into the world, both literally and spiritually.

Gregory of Nyssa argued that the fall resulted from what he called "the disease of love of rule."[2] The devil, when tempting Adam and Eve, was subject to this disease, which according to Gregory was the primary and fundamental cause of all the evil that followed. Gregory, like Augustine a generation later, thus identifies pride and the pursuit of power as what we now call the "original sin." The fall, in other words, introduces divisions into human nature as people arrogate themselves to be judges and masters over one another. Sin is not so much a property of individuals as it is about broken relations. Death enters the world as human nature is divided against itself because of the "disease of love of rule." The result is that humanity is now made subject to death. Adam must work hard in order to barely survive (Gen 3:17–19). Morality—the knowledge of good and evil—alienates humanity from God, but it also alienates humanity from nature. Because of sin, the relationship of humans with creation becomes a matter of fighting for survival. Work, as William Stringfellow explained it in twentieth-century terms, represents the broken relationship between humans and the rest of creation. Nature has become objectified, while humans are alienated from God, creation, and each other.

Much has been made of the story of the brothers Cain and Abel as being a story of stages in the establishment of human civilization. Abel was a shepherd, while Cain worked the soil (Gen 4:2). Cain killed his brother Abel, whom he believed was unjustly

2. Gregory of Nyssa, *Catechetical Discourse* 23.

favored by God. Murder is the first concrete act of sin. By killing his brother, Cain makes himself the judge of life and death, a right that belongs only to God. When God offers to protect Cain on the condition that he will live as a nomad without a permanent home, Cain refuses and instead builds the first city. Civilization, as Jacques Ellul explained in his *The Meaning of the City*, is, at its core, humanity's attempt to gain security by building its own solid walls—rather than relying on God's protective mercy. Politics (from the Greek word for "city," *polis*) is fundamentally a matter of taking control of human life by establishing an order of power without God. Politics is as such humanity's "No!" to God.

The long story that follows is a drama of human disobedience and God's judgment. Much of the biblical narrative deals with the negative consequences of human sin, violence, domination, and injustice. The flood, for example, is a divine response to human evil: "The earth was corrupt before God, and the earth was filled with violence" (Gen 6:11). The violence originated from the fall had infected all creation. When God purges the earth, the purpose is to restore it—at least in part—to its original harmonious order. To ensure peace, God makes a new covenant after the flood that emphasizes the infinite value of all humans: "Whoever sheds human blood, by humans shall their blood be shed; for in the image of God has God made humankind" (Gen 9:6). This rule establishes the principle of reciprocity that runs through biblical ethics. Its basis is not abstract law, but an ontological fact about human existence—the dignity of all humans that comes from the fact that humanity is created in the image of God.

Although we have already heard in the account of the creation that humans are made in the image of God, this is the first time in the biblical narrative that the ethical significance of this fact is explicated. Humans are created in the image of God and, as such, are of infinite value, as early Christian theologians would frequently emphasize. The logic of all ethics—reciprocity and mutuality—stems from the fact that all humans equally participate in a common humanity that reflects the infinite value of God. In Genesis, the principle of reciprocity is formulated negatively ("whoever sheds human blood, by humans shall their blood be shed"). However, as Tertullian (c. 160–225) argued, it nevertheless anticipates Jesus' positive principle of doing to others what we would like others to do to us.[3] The principle of mutual retribution limits the dynamics of revenge that would otherwise escalate and get out of control and lead to the victory of the strong over the weak. To this extent, it foreshadows a coming state of affairs in which violence is abolished altogether.

While all humans reflect the goodness of God by being created in God's image, it is also made clear in the story in Genesis that "the human heart was only evil all the time" (Gen 6:5) and that "every inclination of the human heart is evil from childhood" (Gen 8:21). This is often understood in terms of "hereditary sin," but the point could also be made that humans are inevitably born into social structures of power and domination, judgmentalism, and violence. These structures make it impossible for us not to participate in the injustice that pervades the world. Perhaps the two are sides of the same coin. The personal identity of humans cannot be understood independently of their relations. We are never free-floating individuals, but always embedded in particular historical and cultural contexts.

According to the Septuagint translation (the Greek version of the Bible used by early Christians), when God divided humanity, he "set the boundaries of the nations according to the number of the angels of God" (Deut 32:8). Following the first-century Jewish philosopher Philo of Alexandria, early Christians such as Clement of Alexandria (c. 150–215) pointed out that God had assigned guardian angels to give each nation its peculiar characteristics. The purpose, he believed, was to prepare each nation in its own way for Christ.[4] Since people(s) are different, they need different pedagogical means, so to speak.

The importance of cultural distinctives is evident in the story of the Tower of Babel. The point of the story is not so much that humanity wants to reach heaven by its own works—that is part

3. Tertullian, *Against Marcion* 4, 16.

4. Clement of Alexandria, *Stromateis* 7, 2; 6, 4.

of the story—but the real point is that the builders want to gain complete independence by creating "a name" for themselves (Gen 11:4). In building the Tower of Babel, humanity repeats the sin of Adam and Eve by attempting to be its own god, judging and defining humanity. The totalitarian, imperial project of creating a completely coherent, all-encompassing totality and unity under one rule inevitably turns into devastation. Humanity's attempt at making a unifying name for itself results in its shattering and fragmentation into diversity and multiplicity.

However, as suggested by Clement, this diversity may not, however, be all bad. The diversity of languages, national customs and moral norms, reflects the fact, also explained by Origen, that each nation has been given a guardian angel who gives each nation its particular characteristics.[5] From a "modern" perspective this need not be understood mythologically or in "essentialist" terms. It simply reflects the fact that being human in a divided world means being subject to circumstances. This fact is in and of itself neutral. Humanity is divided into cultures, nations, particular identities of all sorts.

In the Bible, one such people is Israel. In itself, Israel is no different from other nations, but in relation to God it has the peculiar status of being the chosen people. The liberation from slavery in Egypt and the call to freedom under God is the narrative that defines the identity of the Jewish people. This is the narrative that is presupposed as the background for the Decalogue. The Ten Commandments are not a set of abstract moral norms or laws, but a description of the *ethos* that must characterize Israel as God's freed people in its particular historical context.

When Israel in the First Book of Samuel demands to have a king like other nations, God makes it clear that this demand is in fact apostasy (1 Sam 8:7). The chosen people are not to be ruled by secular powers, and in this lies its freedom. When Israel is nevertheless granted a king, with all the hierarchical authority implied by monarchy, this is clearly a compromise. As Jacques Ellul noted, the story shows that since political authority rests on defiance and

5. Origen, *Against Celsus* 5,30.

the rejection of God, it can only be dictatorial, abusive, and unjust. But even as Israel in its secular ambitions repeatedly turns away from God, God remains faithful. Israel carries the hope of a future realization of God's kingdom, where God will "judge the nations," as the prophecies of Isaiah put it (Isa 2:4). This "judgment" is not only to be understood in a negative sense, but will result in peace for the nations as they "beat their swords into plowshares."

True religion is understood in much of the prophetic tradition, exemplified by Isaiah, as righteousness and justice. While Israel as a nation is defined by its religious customs, it often turns out that God is not interested in piety for its own sake: "The kind of fasting I want is this: to remove the chains of oppression and the yoke of injustice, and to let the oppressed go free" (Isa 58:6). There is obviously no religion here confined to a private, individual piety or anything like a modern Protestant idea of "justification by faith alone." There is only a clear call to "do away with the yoke of oppression, with the pointing finger and malicious talk" and to "spend yourselves in behalf of the hungry and satisfy the needs of the oppressed." This is the only way to make "your light rise in the darkness" (Isa 58:9–10).

Those who pursue justice, says Isaiah, will "rebuild the ancient ruins" and "raise up the age-old foundations" (Isa 58:12). Social justice is not just an optional addendum to personal piety, but integral to the restoration of creation shattered by human evil, violence, and injustice. The Sabbath, for example, is not a meaningless religious requirement, but a celebration of the freedom from work and slavery that God made possible when freeing Israel from Egypt. The Sabbath is an act of both resistance and an alternative, said Walter Brueggemann, as it makes it clear that God's people are not commodities in the service of production, but humans situated in an "economy of neighborliness." For early Christians, like Tertullian, the "temporal Sabbath" prefigured the "eternal Sabbath" in which Christians abstain from "all servile work."[6] In this way, the people who truly keeps the Sabbath is a sign of the coming kingdom of God. The Sabbath is not only a commemoration of

6. Tertullian, *An Answer to the Jews* 4.

freedom, but also an anticipation of a final restoration in which creation as such will be freed from the bondage of labor, violence, and domination.

It is, of course, also in Isaiah that we find the prophecy of "the suffering servant," who would bring righteousness by bearing our sins (Isa 53:5). The kingdom that will restore creation is not the work of a majestic king or powerful political projects, but comes through the work of the absolute outsider: "He was despised, and we esteemed him not" (Isa 53:3). God brings justice through the powerless. According to the traditional rabbinic reading of Isaiah, the suffering servant is Israel, the Jewish people, who suffers in the world in order to serve God. While not denying this, the Christian tradition, beginning with the New Testament, has centered this claim on one specific person—Jesus Christ. He is the suffering servant that will "justify many." This justice is not only an extrinsic justification of the sinner. The suffering servant brings real justice for the poor, the oppressed, the hungry, and the outsiders, if we are to believe Isaiah. That this is also the message of the New Testament becomes clear when we understand the story of Jesus through the prophetic tradition. It is also clear, however, that the kingdom of God is very different from whatever ideals of justice we may hold.

II.

The Immanence of the Kingdom

He has performed mighty deeds with his arm;
he has scattered those who are proud in their inmost thoughts.
He has brought down rulers from their thrones
but has lifted up the humble.
He has filled the hungry with good things
but has sent the rich away empty.

—MARY'S SONG IN LUKE 1:46–55

IN Jesus' day, Babel was a story of the past. The empire in power was now Rome. This is the political setting of the Christmas story. Mary and Joseph are traveling to the town of Bethlehem as the emperor had called for a census to "register the whole world" (Luke 2:1–5). This was, of course, an obvious exercise of imperial power—and perhaps not of the morally neutral or irrelevant sort that it might at first seem. When King David did something similar by counting the Israelites, it was considered a great sin (1 Chr 21). While it is not exactly clear why David's census was a sin, one plausible explanation could be that David was thereby repeating the sin of Babel—trying to master and dominate people by naming or numbering them. And now Rome is doing the same thing.

In the Gospel according to Luke, the story of Jesus is preceded by the story of Mary's pregnancy. When Mary heard the surprising news of her pregnancy, she praised the Lord, who had "brought down the mighty from their thrones," but "exalted the lowly" and "filled the hungry," while sending "the rich away empty" (Luke 1:46–55). The Christmas narrative, though often subject to glittery and idyllic imagery, is already loaded with political significance. Mary is about to give birth to a Savior who will restore justice and righteousness. The new king, however, is born in poverty on the outskirts of human civilization. Jesus is the Suffering Servant from his birth, even if his active ministry only begins when he is baptized by John in the desert.

John was the last of the great prophets, taking his cue from Isaiah's words about the "voice of one crying in the wilderness: Prepare the way for the Lord." John proclaimed "the good news" (Luke 3:18), even if judgment seems to have been at the forefront of his ministry. His harsh criticism of material inequality and the abuse of power was a call to righteousness and social justice: "Anyone who has two shirts should share with the one who has none, and anyone who has food should do the same" (Luke 3:11). As a call to repentance, John's message was fundamentally about preparing for the coming of God's kingdom.

When Jesus approached John, it was—obviously—not because he needed to "repent." This is clear from John's reluctance to baptize him, but Jesus insists that by doing so they will "fulfill all righteousness" (Matt 3:15). What makes Jesus' baptism by John so significant is that it anticipates his suffering, which is also referred to as a "baptism" (Luke 12:50). This is the "baptism" that effectively fulfills all righteousness, because it is the means by which Jesus puts a stop to the unrighteousness of the world and makes the kingdom of God present.

The political significance of Jesus' ministry becomes clear already when, after being baptized, he continues into the desert to be tempted by the devil—literally "the slanderer." The story that played out when Adam and Eve were tempted to gain knowledge of good and evil is partly repeated in Jesus' temptations in the desert. In both cases the temptation is to gain control and power. Significantly, the devil's claim to have been given all the power and glory of all the kingdoms of the world, is not refuted by Jesus (Luke 4:6), but Jesus simply refuses to serve the slanderer in order to have a share in his power. This is fundamentally the refusal of "state power" (Peterson). The fact that Jesus does not make use of ordinary political means already makes it clear that the kingdom of God is not of this world.

Having refused the devil's temptations, Jesus can now proclaim the immanence of the kingdom: "The kingdom of God is at hand, repent and believe the good news!" (Mark 1:15). By refusing to make use of political power, Jesus has opened an alternative way and made the kingdom immanent. The immanence (literally *at-hand-ness*) of the kingdom is the core of the gospel, the "good news." It takes faith, however, to perceive the kingdom. Because the kingdom of God is radically different from kingdoms based on power and domination, we need to repent in order to recognize it. Repentance (*metanoia* in Greek) literally means to "think over." Jesus' proclamation is not a threat, but a call to see reality in the new light of the kingdom. This is the beginning of faith. We cannot see and understand the realities of the kingdom through our usual categories shaped by concepts of power and domination.

But what is "the kingdom of God"? No clear definition is given. Jesus speaks of his kingdom almost exclusively in parables. Early Christian theologians understood the need for parables to follow from fundamental theological truths. God, who is radically different from the world, is ineffable and incomprehensible, and so is the kingdom of God. Clement of Alexandria, for example, explained that things that cannot be mastered by language must be spoken of in symbolic language. For similar reasons, Gregory of Nyssa explained in a sermon on the Lord's Prayer that it is only to ease communication that we call the kingdom of God a "kingdom." Unlike all other kingdoms, Gregory argued, the kingdom of God does not work through force or the kind of tyrannical power that enforces the obedience of its subjects through compulsion.[1] Virtue must be free from fear so that the good may be chosen voluntarily.

1. Gregory of Nyssa, *On the Lord's Prayer* 3, 256.

In other words, the kingdom of God must be described "apophatically," that is, by "unsaying" the way things function in the world. This was the point when Nicolai Berdyaev—as mentioned above—described the kingdom of God as "anarchy." The "religious truth of anarchism," he argued, is "a truth of apophatics."[2] We can only point to God. With our rational language we exercise power over the world. We dominate things, nature, and other people by categorizing and boxing up things with our concepts. This is not in itself sinful—Adam was given the task of naming the animals—but rational language becomes sinful when we use it for controlling our relationships with each other and God. The kingdom of God, however, eschews such linguistic domination, which is why it can only be approached in parables and symbolic language.

The kingdom of God is hidden, it moves and grows subversively, yet it is all-embracing. This seems to be the point when in a parable Jesus compares the kingdom to a mustard seed that grows into a great tree that can house all the birds of the sky (Mark 4:30–32). It is not the first time that a kingdom has been compared to a tree. Think of the Babylonian king Nebuchadnezzar's strange dream about a huge tree visible to the ends of the earth. The tree symbolized Nebuchadnezzar's imperial rule, but it is cut down by a "messenger coming down from heaven," much like the Tower of Babel before him (Dan 4:13). Jesus' parable seems to draw on these images, but his prophecy about the kingdom of God is different. A mustard seed does not normally grow into a tree—a bush, at most. However, by its humility and subversive nonviolence, the kingdom of God accomplishes what all other kingdoms and empires had failed to accomplish before. The kingdom of God achieves the final unity of all reality by making a home for all the "birds of the sky." It does so, however, not by forcing what is different and "other" into uniformity, but by embracing all distinctives into a harmonious whole.

"The coming of the kingdom of God is not something that can be observed," says Jesus (Luke 17:20). The kingdom of God is a matter of relations, just as the Trinitarian God is essentially

2. Berdyaev, *Slavery and Freedom*, 148.

relational, although not in a way that can be made explicit or definable in finite terms. While Tolstoy made much of Jesus' famous saying that "the kingdom of God is within you" (Luke 17:21), it is probably more accurate to translate the saying as, "the kingdom of God is in your midst." The kingdom of God is not about some private, religious "spirituality," but a matter of human relationships. The kingdom is the person of Jesus himself—in Greek, the *autobasileia* (Origen)—who has come in our midst to reshape our way of being in the world. The kingdom of God is present wherever Jesus is present, not as a political order, but as the work of God in the person of Christ.

As early Christians saw it, the immanence of the kingdom fulfilled the prophecy of nations beating their swords into plowshares (Isa 2:4). It is the Word of God preached by the apostles, Irenaeus explained, that causes the nations to abandon their violent ways.[3] The kingdom of God works in ways quite different from those known to the political powers of this world. This is repeatedly illustrated by the attitude and practice of Jesus. A good example is when, before Easter, Jesus enters the gates of Jerusalem on a donkey rather than a proud, white warrior horse. This is a clear sign—almost too clear—that Jesus does not base his rule on violence and power, but on humility and service. We expected a king, but not one who would be humble and powerless. Jesus takes on the role of the Suffering Servant, the outsider who will bring about justice and peace through service rather than political power.

Jesus denied being a king in the sense that the crowd expected, Origen noted, but he declared the superiority of his kingdom when he said that if his kingdom was of this world, his servants would fight for it (John 18:36).[4] In other words, the superiority of the kingdom of God is expressed precisely in the fact that it does not need to be established by violence. The kingdom of God is not "of this world" (John 18:36). Jesus makes this clear after being arrested and handed over to Pilate. Now, as Walter Wink has pointed out, the word "world" can mean many things. The Greek word

3. Irenaeus, *Against Heresies* 4,4.

4. Origen, *Against Celsus* 1,61.

cosmos means world, but it can also mean world order or even just the order of things. The "prince of this world" (John 12:31) is the principle of violence and domination—the *archê*—that characterizes the present world order. The kingdom of God is not a part of this world order but something completely different. It is not, however, "otherworldly" in the sense of being *outside* the world or in a different world altogether. The kingdom is "not of this world," but it has become immanent in the presence of Christ.

The immanence of the kingdom had become discernible through signs already when Jesus healed the sick and forgave people their sins. Less spectacular from our point of view, though perhaps not so in the eyes of first-century people, is that Jesus had fellowship with sinners. He even eats with them. By having fellowship with all kinds of people without distinction, Jesus reconciles the shattered pieces of fragmented humanity. This is the "political" meaning of the Lord's Supper—it may well be a mystical participation in Christ, as held by traditional theology, but its primary significance comes from the narratives about Christ's reconciling fellowship with people of all kinds.

But how are we to understand the "immanence" or "at-handness" of the kingdom? An important point about the immanence of the kingdom is that it really *is* present. It is not just an ideal or a plan for us to realize, but it breaks into the world in paradoxical and surprising ways. This was a point made in twentieth-century dialectical theology with roots in the radical preaching of Christoph Blumhardt. "Jesus is Victor!" was the motto of this movement. The kingdom of God runs counter to all "religion" and individualistic piety. Our struggle for the kingdom is only possible because the kingdom is already immanent. Humans—including the church—cannot make the kingdom their property. Salvation is not only about the afterlife, but just as much about the here and now. That the kingdom is immanent means that it is tangible, it is actually present, close at hand. Still, it is so in a way that is not clearly visible, it requires faith to perceive the presence of the kingdom. This is perhaps why there is always the temptation to turn the kingdom into a project, something that is to be realized through human power and control. It is, however, only when we admit our inability to produce the kingdom by our own means that we can actually become aware of its presence.

This is why the kingdom belongs to the children, as Jesus makes clear (Luke 18:15–17). Not because they are pure or innocent, as if that was a condition for salvation, but because they do not pretend to be capable of mastering the kingdom. Since the kingdom of God is not attained by power as we know it, only the powerless are capable of recognizing it. The "power of the powerless" is the name of the true God, said Jürgen Moltmann. In reality, however, we are all powerless. Faith is simply a matter of recognizing our lack of power. To make this recognition is also beyond our power, which is why faith in the gospel is not something that we can choose to exercise by will. Faith is only possible as a product of having heard the message about the kingdom. Repentance means being brought to think in new ways that make it possible to perceive the presence of the kingdom. In this sense, repentance is not a moral term, although it can of course include remorse and regret. The new way of life that follows from having recognized the presence of the kingdom is not itself repentance, but a product of it (Matt 3:8). In other words, the ethics of the kingdom presupposes the good news of its immanence. But while the kingdom eschews all definition, the practice that marks its presence may be subject to ethical discernment. Having made this clear, we can now move on to the ethical teachings of Jesus.

The Ethics of the Kingdom

Blessed are the poor in spirit,
 for theirs is the kingdom of heaven.
Blessed are those who mourn,
 for they will be comforted.
Blessed are the meek,
 for they will inherit the earth.
Blessed are those who hunger and thirst for righteousness,
 for they will be filled.
Blessed are the merciful,
 for they will be shown mercy.
Blessed are the pure in heart,
 for they will see God.
Blessed are the peacemakers,
 for they will be called children of God.
Blessed are those who are persecuted because of righteousness,
 for theirs is the kingdom of heaven.

—THE BEATITUDES FROM JESUS' SERMON ON THE MOUNT (MATTHEW 5:3–12)

JESUS' ethical teachings are perhaps best known from his Sermon on the Mount. Here we have the Golden Rule, the Lord's Prayer, and the Beatitudes that introduce the sermon. As is clear from the beginning, the Beatitudes, like the rest of the sermon, revolve around the kingdom of God—or the kingdom of "heaven," which is arguably synonymous. While the Beatitudes have often been understood to exemplify personal piety, their political significance seems clear from the beginning.

"Blessed are the poor in spirit," says Jesus, "for theirs is the kingdom of heaven." Traditionally, poverty of spirit has been understood as humility. Humility (from *humilitas* in Latin) is literally a matter of recognizing that we are made of clay (or "dust," Gen 2:7). To be humble is to be grounded. While this may not in itself seem like a "political" claim, it could easily be applied critically against the powerful. Gregory of Nyssa, for example, in a sermon on spiritual poverty and humility, took the beatitude as a cue for criticizing people who exalt themselves above others because of their political office.[1] Those, he argued, who "strut on the stage of life" because of imperial office, "regularly overstep the boundaries of human nature." People of power mistakenly assume divine power and authority when they think themselves sovereign over human life. But, Gregory asks, "how can anyone be the master of someone else's life, when he is not even the master of his own life?" The powerful should become poor in spirit by looking to Jesus who voluntarily became poor for our sake. Those in power should look with respect to other humans who are "by nature our equals"—and not inflict injury on others as a result of that "mistaken masquerade of government," as Gregory puts it.

While this may not completely delegitimize power and authority altogether, these comments are a strong reminder that following the example of Jesus should lead to recognizing the equal worth of all people. All domination and violence that results from "the deception of power" is contrary to the humility pertaining to the kingdom. This is why, we might add, Jesus can warn his disciples not to "exercise authority" over one another as the rulers of the nations do (Matt 20:25–28). Instead, they are to serve one another as Jesus did. We do not become blessed by seeking to imitate God's majesty or sovereignty, Gregory noted in his sermon, but we can imitate God's Word that has become human for our

1. Gregory of Nyssa, *On the Beatitudes* 1, 6–7.

sake. To imitate God is, in other words, to be truly human like Christ was. We have communion with God, says Gregory, when we have communion with the poor and powerless, as Jesus did. Through humility, the poor in spirit receive the kingdom of heaven here and now.

There is, according to Gregory of Nyssa, a logical order in the Beatitudes. From humility follows meekness—"blessed are the meek"—which again makes righteousness, mercy, and peace possible. Righteousness (or "justice") is not a principle that can be used to form a particular kind of political order, Gregory explains.[2] For example, if we make righteousness a matter of judging or distributing wealth according to merit, it will presuppose an unequal distribution of power, and thereby refute itself. Those who "hunger" for righteousness are simply those who seek God, says Gregory. True righteousness in other words deconstructs whatever simplistic notions we have of political justice. This does not, of course, mean that true righteousness is irrelevant for how we relate to people. Participating in the Word means pursuing the justice, mercy, and peace that comes from Christ.

"Blessed are the peacemakers," says Jesus—or literally "the pacifists" (from *pacifici* in Latin). Pacifism is not the same as passivity or indifference in the face of evil. Pacifism means actively working for peace. It is those who make peace whom Jesus calls "children of God." Children of God, according to the Sermon on the Mount, are people who are "perfect" like their "heavenly father" (Matt 5:48). Perfection does not mean perfectionism. It simply means to refuse, like God, to make distinctions between people. God "causes his sun to rise on the evil and the good and rains on the just and the unjust" (Matt 5:45). God's children are those who like God love their enemies and pray for those who persecute them (Matt 5:43).

Early Christians, for example Irenaeus, understood the prophecy of Isaiah about the nations that would "forge their swords into plowshares and their spears into pruning hooks" as fulfilled

2. Gregory of Nyssa, *On the Beatitudes* 4, 112.

with Jesus and the church.[3] Justin Martyr explained that "we who were busy fighting and slaughtering each other have replaced our weapons with the justice, philanthropy, faith and hope that we have from the Crucified."[4] Tertullian is famous for saying that "when the Lord disarmed Peter, he thereby disarmed every soldier."[5] Peter briefly tried his hand at violent resistance when Jesus was captured in Gethsemane. Jesus himself had encouraged the disciples to get swords, but, it seems, only to have the opportunity to make it clear that they should refrain from using them: "Everyone who takes up a sword will fall by the sword," he says (Matt 26:52), and so Jesus disarmed every soldier. "How can a Christian serve as a soldier," Tertullian asks rhetorically, "when Jesus has taken the sword from him?" For Clement of Alexandria, Christian pacifism was linked to Jesus' admonition not to worry (Matt 6:25–30). "It is not in war that we are trained, but in peace," he notes.[6] War, like excessive wealth, requires preparation and worry, but peace and love require neither weapons nor preparation. The Word is enough to sustain them. Christ has gathered an army of "soldiers of peace" who shed no blood. Origen agreed, and argued that it is forbidden for Christians to take the life of anyone under any circumstances.[7]

While throughout history the Beatitudes have often been seen as not meant for the ordinary believer, early Christians often emphasized the importance of the Sermon on the Mount for the Christian life here and now. The Beatitudes describe a radically alternative way of being in the world as the kingdom of God (or "kingdom of heaven") has become immanent. It may be added, however, that the Beatitudes are prophetical words, not moral ideals—they are good news about the kingdom of God for those who mourn and long for righteousness. In the Beatitudes, Jesus does not come with "threatening demands," noted Martin Luther, but "with pleasant promises." Such a classically Protestant corrective

3. Irenaeus, *Against Heresies* 4, 4.
4. Justin Martyr, *First Apology* 39.
5. Tertullian, *Of Idolatry* 19.
6. Clement of Alexandria, *The Instructor* 1, 12.
7. Origen, *Against Celsus* 8, 73.

should be made to a tradition that has too often made the kingdom of God into something to be achieved by human means. The teachings of Jesus should not be transformed into yet another system of religious rules and observances.

Much can be made of Jesus' opposition to the imperial authorities, but Jesus was just as opposed to the religious authorities of his day: the highly religious who wanted to substitute one kind of power for another by imposing all kinds of moral rules on people. Jesus may seem to be sharpening the law ("you have heard that it was said, but . . ."), but in doing so he takes the law out of the control of the Scribes. God's law is not a tool to be used for judging others. The critical attitude toward the religious elite is evident throughout the Sermon on the Mount. This should remind us that an attitude shaped by the "anarchy" of the kingdom should lead to a critical attitude to whatever religious groups who divide the world into, for example, "clean" and "unclean," "infidels" and the "faithful." The ethics of the kingdom is not a subspecies of "religious" ethics in general, but a radical alternative.

There is at the core of the gospel a critical attitude to religion, much of which is related to its opposition to power and domination. Early Christians, not unlike modern critics of religion, often saw idolatry as an attempt to absolutize human customs and relations of domination. Lactantius (c. 250–325) explained that when the mutual communion between humans has been broken, it was due to ignorance of the true God as the common origin of all.[8] When humans began to worship a multiplicity of idols, the result was the dissolution of community, and might became right. Christianity, on the other hand, exposes idolatry as an expression of human self-assertion and the desire for power in order to restore the natural reciprocity and community between people.

We may add that while a religious idea of "God" is often supposed to be the guarantor of morality, the reverse is often true: it is precisely when we can justify our desire for power in terms of "the will of God" that we become truly capable of transgressing common moral norms. As Pascal observed, people do evil with the

8. Lactantius, *Epitome of the Divine Institutes* 59.

greatest pleasure precisely when they do it with a clear conscience. To legitimize one's morality and way of life with reference to God, instead of taking responsibility for one's choices and actions, is to take God's name "in vain" (Exod 20:7). Again, we cannot simply take Jesus' teachings about the kingdom of God as yet another example of religious teachings comparable with others.

Jesus does not come with yet another religious system that must be observed in order to please God, but to set people free. The Sermon on the Mount is not a system of religious morals and rules. This is clear from what Jesus says about observances such as fasting and prayer. When Jesus teaches his disciples how to pray and fast, this should not be understood as a new set of rules for religious observance. Rather, Jesus' teachings can be understood dialectically, as the negation of religious norms. Jesus makes it clear that prayer and fasting should be "hidden" and private (Matt 6:5–6) in *distinction* to how the religious act in public. These things should not become ways of exercising religious power and authority over others. The relationship with God that is the purpose of religious practice is not a matter of rigid rules.

Paul makes this equally clear when he says that our beliefs about such things should be a matter between the individual and God (Rom 14:13–23). The kingdom of God, he says, "is not a matter of eating and drinking, but of righteousness, peace and joy in the Holy Spirit." This is why we should not judge each other because of differences in religious practice. In his Sermon on the Mount, Jesus is even more radical in forbidding his disciples to judge in general: "Do not judge, or you too will be judged" (Matt 7:1). By forbidding his disciples to judge *and* condemn (Luke 6:37), he negates the core of human pride and sinfulness. If eating from the tree of knowledge of good and evil meant the introduction of judgmentalism and moralism in human relations, not judging means rooting out any kind of judgmental attitude that leads people to exalt themselves above others.

This means that we cannot make the ethical teachings of Jesus into a new law that can be used to judge others. Instead of judging others, we should see ourselves *in* the other. This is the positive point already latent in the negative ethics of reciprocity that first appeared in the story of Noah as a prohibition of murder (Gen 9:6). In Jesus' teachings this ethics is now translated into an explicitly positive requirement to treat others as we would like to be treated—the principle also known as the Golden Rule (Matt 7:12; Luke 6:31). In fact, this principle is the basis for the entire law and the prophets, says Jesus. The entire ethical teaching of the Sermon on the Mount should be understood as functions of the Golden Rule—examples of what it means to treat others in terms of positive, anticipative reciprocity.

Following the Golden Rule is a matter of love. Love is the foundation of the law, which, as Paul puts it, means that whoever loves others has fulfilled the entire law (Rom 13:10). Christian "love" is not a warm, fuzzy feeling of compassion or some erotic desire for what we lack, but is *agape*, charity or care. Love does not seek to dominate its object, nor does it sacrifice the concrete person for some higher ideal. It is not impersonal or anonymous, but consists in reciprocal relations—as for example Clement of Alexandria explained, when he described love as directed toward building actual community.[9] While it is often noted that most religions and cultures share some sort of reciprocal ethics similar to the Golden Rule, it was only with early Christianity that this was formulated in positive terms of treating others as we would want to be treated—rather than in negative terms of *not* treating others as we would *not* want to be treated. The widespread negative definition of the Golden Rule does, however, seem to foreshadow the positive and truly universal version preached by Jesus in the Sermon on the Mount.

In the second century, Tertullian wrote against Marcion that Christians had been taught to live by a universal ethics. This universal ethics already existed at the core of Jewish law, but it was only fully expressed with Jesus' universal requirement to treat others as one would like to be treated.[10] Justin Martyr explained that Christians have abandoned the norms and traditions of

9. E.g., Clement of Alexandria, *The Instructor* 2,12. More on this below.

10. Tertullian, *Against Marcion* 4,16.

human culture that overshadow our natural awareness of universal ethical truths. Christians live by the Golden Rule, which requires us to love our neighbor. Should there be any doubt as to who our "neighbor" is, Justin explained that our neighbor is "no other than the thinking life that has the same feelings as ourselves, the human person."[11]

While the Golden Rule is based on a universal ethical concern for reciprocity and care for others, its positive demand for love comes to the fore only with the immanence of the kingdom of God in Jesus. The Golden Rule is, to this extent, "the new law of righteousness," to borrow a term from the seventeenth-century radical Gerrard Winstanley—even if it points back to the community of love and freedom in which we were originally intended to participate. For Winstanley, the point of the Golden Rule was that the basis of morality is our own will, not foreign principles that are authoritatively imposed on us. Christian ethics, then—to the extent that we can use that term at all—is not about obeying abstract divine commandments, but about participating in the freedom and love of Christ by loving others as ourselves (Mark 12:31).

This insistence on human autonomy is not just something "modern." The Golden Rule, argued John Chrysostom (c. 347–407) already in the fourth century, is not some strange law that surpasses our nature, but something that requires autonomous judgment: "Let your own will be the law," said Chrysostom, "become yourself the judge, the lawgiver of your own life: Do you wish to be loved? Love!"[12] The Golden Rule sets us free to decide what that means in everyday practice. The Golden Rule liberates us from abstract moral norms in order to make real community possible. While shared precepts for conduct can be useful and even necessary in practice, we are free to judge the extent to which they help promote the love and freedom of the kingdom.

"Christ is not under law," wrote Origen, but Christ is "the fulfillment of the law." Christ is truth and life itself, but he also is the law itself. Those who are united to Christ are, as such, not

11. Justin Martyr, *Dialogue with Trypho* 93.

12. John Chrysostom, *Homilies on the Statues* 13,7.

under law, Origen continued, "but are *themselves* law."[13] This does not mean that Christians are "lawless," but that they live in accordance with the peace and freedom that pertains to Christ. The Word of God is "the law of liberty," said Irenaeus, when he noticed how the gospel had established peace where it had been accepted.[14] This "liberty" is not to be confused with modern liberal notions of freedom. Freedom cannot be reduced to the individual right to do whatever one pleases, as long as this does not interfere with the freedom of others. In the modern individualist conception of freedom (shared by "liberals" and "conservatives" alike), people are fundamentally seen as competitors. From the Christian perspective, however, freedom is a matter of acknowledging the dignity that we share with the concrete person, our "neighbor." For this reason, the kingdom of God cannot be translated into an abstract idea of universal human rights.

The conservative may have a point, then, in that Christian love is a matter of loving one's neighbor as a concrete person, not as an abstract ideal. This does not mean, however, that we can structure love hierarchically in an "order of love." When, for example, Gregory of Nyssa and Augustine talked of an "order of love," the point was that we should love God first, and then love whomever we happen to encounter, be it family, neighbor, strangers, or even enemies.[15] We may not be capable of doing this, but this is nevertheless the order that belongs to the kingdom. The Christian "order of love" is no order at all in the worldly sense, but only "apophatically" so. The kingdom exists at a deeper level, beyond any order by which we try to dominate and limit the love of God. This, however, is also why the kingdom may surprisingly permeate human relations, despite our attempts to set limits.

The freedom and dignity of the concrete person are also the basis for understanding Jesus' approach to nonviolence in the Sermon on the Mount. Jesus famously tells his disciples to turn the other cheek when someone strikes them on the right cheek (Matt

13. Origen, *Commentary on Romans* 3,6,5.

14. Irenaeus, *Against Heresies* 4,4.

15. Gregory of Nyssa, *On the Song of Songs* 122.

5:39). As some theologians have argued, this does not mean passive submission to authority. In fact, turning the other cheek may be considered a form of nonviolent resistance.[16] The purpose of such nonviolent resistance is not, however, to assert one's rights against those of the perpetrator. The purpose must be to insist on the equal dignity of both victim and offender, dissolving these categories altogether.

The principle of positive reciprocity in the Golden Rule—doing to others as we would have them do to us—is arguably also the key to understanding Jesus' approach to possessions and wealth. "Give to everyone who asks of you," says Jesus in the Sermon on the Mount (Matt 5:42). While there may be some truth in Augustine's addition, "but not everything they ask," there is something clearly unconditional about Jesus' statement. We are not to judge whether people are "truly needy." Rather, we are to recognize that we should give because what we have is not our own, but belongs to all in common. This was seen clearly by Clement of Alexandria, when he argued that since God has made everything for all, everything is common, and the rich should not grasp a greater share.[17] In Clement's day, there was apparently an expression that said, "I own something, and have more than enough, so should I not enjoy it?" Clement, however, argues that this way of thinking does not live up to the commandment of neighborly love. He suggests instead that we live by the saying, "I have something, why should I not share it with those in need?" True community—or *koinonia* in Greek—is possible, Clement argued, only when we realize that participating in Christ means entering into the mutual relations of love established by God.

This line of thought was followed by theologians in the fourth century. John Chrysostom famously argued that theft is not only stealing from others, but also failing to share one's possessions with those in need. It may be a stretch to conclude that "property is theft," to quote the French proto-anarchist Pierre-Joseph

16. According to Walter Wink, turning the left cheek requires the offender to use a flat hand for hitting, which was considered a sign of equal dignity.

17. Clement of Alexandria, *The Instructor* 2,12.

Proudhon, but there is a clear notion in the Christian tradition that we only have the right to use what we need. Basil of Caesarea (c. 330–379) argued in a sermon that those who could clothe the naked, but do not, are in fact thieves: "The money which you hoard up," says Basil, "belongs to the poor." This is also why Ambrose of Milan (c. 340–397) could argue that when you give of your possessions to the poor, you are not giving a "gift" to the poor. You are only giving what already belongs to the poor.

In other words: Do not cling to your possessions, they are not yours. The truly radical thing is to get rid of the idea that we have absolute rights to our property. This also means that any struggle for social justice in light of the kingdom must be a matter of solidarity rather than unequal relations of benevolence. We may give away some of "our" money to feel good about ourselves, but in that case we easily end up turning the poor into means for our own moral self-gratification. Hoarding up money and clinging to possessions—in short, greed—is idolatry (Col 3:5), but as Jesus reminds us in the Sermon on the Mount, it is not possible to serve both God and Mammon (Matt 6:24). Jesus is arguably not just talking about getting your priorities straight—the point is not that it's "okay" to pursue wealth and money if you just go to church on Sundays. Jesus is saying that you will necessarily have a negative attitude to money and material wealth if you love God—and *vice versa*.

Origen wrote that "we should rather dishonor the law of Mammon than the law of God."[18] The "law of Mammon" can be understood as the economic rationality that shapes our attempts at securing ourselves materially—the "worries" that we ought to abolish according to the Sermon on the Mount (Matt 6:25). All this does not mean that material goods are of no use, but they should be "despised" to the extent that they become idols, "gods" that rule our lives and come to determine our identity and relations through a purely economic rationality.

Jesus' admonition to "give back to Caesar what is Caesar's and to God what is God's" is not a principle of the separation of religion

18. Origen, *Against Celsus* 8,56.

and politics, but, as Tertullian argued, a demand that we give ourselves to God in whose image we are created.[19] Participating in the freedom of the kingdom of God is only possible when our identity is not determined by political-economic structures and the social norms that support them. Gregory of Nyssa lamented that "most people look to the customs of their ancestors rather than judging for themselves."[20] As a consequence, people seek "positions of authority and power." This does not mean that "tradition" as such is bad, or that it is possible to live without tradition. The gospel and the sacraments, for example, are also traditions passed on from Jesus through the church. Tradition is only bad when it compels people to prioritize power and wealth over the freedom of the gospel and the love of God. Human traditions are often based on an ethics of achievement and merit. The gospel frees people from such ideology by proclaiming that the kingdom is immanent in spite of our achievements.

Such critique of ideology and tradition is arguably at the heart of Jesus' shocking admonition to "hate your family" (Luke 14:26). Far from recommending some kind of extreme individualism, this is an exhortation to live in the freedom, but also the love, that characterizes the kingdom of God. Often these harsh words are interpreted as simply saying that we should put Jesus first and learn to prioritize. While this is arguably true, it misses the political significance of Jesus' words. Of course, "hating" your family does not mean hating the concrete persons that constitute your family, but it is not just a matter of priorities. Hating your family could be understood more generally as not basing your identity on cultural and social norms. Rather, we are to base our identity and relations to others on the kingdom of God. In this way we become truly free to love the members of our family, exactly because this love is not based upon authoritarian structures, be they religious or economic.

The severity of Jesus' teaching is evident in the story of the rich young man who asks Jesus how to inherit eternal life. When

19. Tertullian, *On Idolatry* 15.

20. Gregory of Nyssa, *On the Song of Songs* 65–66.

Jesus explains to his disciples that "it is easier for a camel to enter the kingdom of heaven than for a rich person" (Luke 18:25), we get the feeling from their reaction that no one is actually poor enough to enter the kingdom: "Then who can be saved?" they ask (Luke 18:26). Obviously, we must leave behind not just some of our baggage, but all ideas and structures of wealth and power. Only then do we become light enough to pass through the gate of the kingdom. This should serve as a reminder of what the Protestant Reformers so often emphasized as the core of the gospel. Jesus' ethics of the kingdom is not an easy solution or a method that we can appropriate in our own projects of self-preservation and salvation. In fact, no human is free enough from spiritual and material attachments to enter the kingdom by their own means. No one is actually not serving Mammon, no one is completely free of worry and material attachments.

We come to a stop here. It turns out that we are all so deeply immersed in unrighteousness and injustice that none of us can claim to be without complicity in the unjust realities of the world. No one is able to enter the kingdom: "With humans this is impossible," says Jesus (Matt 19:26). Entering the kingdom is out of our hands. To paraphrase Karl Barth, no political ideology, no system of power, no revolution, no counter-revolution, not even missionary work or the piety of the church, can make entrance into the kingdom of God humanly possible. But what is impossible with humans, is possible with God (Matt 19:26). This is the good news of the gospel. It also makes it clear, however, that the kingdom of God is not something that is in our power. If it were, it would not be "anarchy." The only thing that can bring us into the kingdom is the total dissolution of power. But this is not humanly possible, since even the most ascetic self-denial is still in some way a work of the human "will to power." Only if God acts do we enter the kingdom. Our job is to be attentive and listen for the kingdom—the Christian life is "action in waiting" (Blumhardt)—in opposition to all worldly and religious demands to take control of our destiny and earn our way into the kingdom.

IV.

The Meaning of the Cross (and the Resurrection!)

One died for all, and therefore all died.

—2 CORINTHIANS 5:14

THE "prince" (or *archôn* in Greek) of this world order will be judged when Jesus is "lifted up from the earth" (John 12:31–32). While being "lifted up" could also be translated as "exalted," it seems clear from the context that Jesus was not speaking about his exaltation to a visibly majestic state. In fact, he spoke about being lifted up on the cross, which is the exact opposite. Jesus is paradoxically exalted in his very humiliation, as Martin Luther emphasized. The cross negates all human ideas of power and glory. The cross is God's final judgment on all human sinfulness, pride, and judgmentalism. The cross is the decisive assault on the structures of authority, power, and domination that characterize the present world order. The "time for judgment" is "now" (John 12:31). The "ruler of this world" is already "driven out" by the cross.

God's glory and power is not, however, simply hidden under the contradiction of the cross, as if it were in reality something other than the cross. The glory and power of God are revealed in the cross, *in* powerlessness, so that we can say that *this* is God, and that God is like *this* (Moltmann). The cross is the "weakness of

God" that overcomes all human strength, and "the foolishness of God" that is wiser than all human wisdom, as Paul famously puts it (1 Cor 1:25). It should come as no surprise, then, that even Jesus' own disciples did not understand what he was up to when he predicted his suffering and death. How could the kingdom of God be established through the shameful death of the king, who died as a criminal and outcast on the cross? But this is how the upside-down kingdom was to become present. The kingdom defies all human standards of politics, all human wisdom, and in many cases even our intuitions of what is just and right.

This can be illustrated by the story about how Jesus, not long after his entrance into Jerusalem, went to Bethany to dine in the house of Simon the Leper (Matt 26:6). As he sat with his disciples, a woman came up to Jesus and poured expensive perfume on his head. The disciples saw this as quite inappropriate. Could this precious oil not have been used for more reasonable purposes? Think of all the money that could have been raised for the poor by selling it, and here she goes wasting it all! But Jesus welcomes the woman and sees a symbolic meaning in her devotion: By anointing him with oil, the woman has anointed Jesus for his coming death. The additional point could be made that when the woman anoints Jesus, she doesn't just anoint him for his death, but also for his kingship. Jesus is the anointed, the Messiah, the king. Or rather, these are two sides of the same coin: it is exactly through his death that Jesus becomes king (or exercises his kingship, if the former sounds too adoptionist). That is why he entered Jerusalem—not to become a secular king or political leader, but to die on the cross. This, however, is exactly what his disciples do not understand. Jesus' disciples seem to have been more concerned about secular justice than the kingdom of God.

We often do the same thing, even if we come to different conclusions. Whatever political conclusions we draw from the stories of Jesus, they will be tainted with ideology and, as such, opposed to the kingdom of God. From a classically "liberal" point of view, we could argue that if the woman owned the perfume, she had every right to do what she wanted with it. Or we could argue from a "progressive" standpoint, like the disciples, that the oil should have been sold and the money given to the poor. But Jesus does not seem to care much about our notions of what is right. Our ideas of right and justice must be negated, crossed out, by dying on the cross with Jesus.

This is not to be understood as a kind of religious nihilism, claiming that there are then no Christian standards of justice at all. Just as Jesus does not remain in the grave, neither should our concepts of justice remain dead. Crucified with Christ, our concepts of justice are deconstructed, but only to be transformed by the cross. The cross unites justice with the self-sacrificial love that is the essence of God and the kingdom. As Origen argued against Gnosticism, the justice and goodness of God are not opposed to each other, but come together in his transforming love for all humanity, realized in the incarnation, death, and resurrection of the Word in Christ.[1] This is why, to understand the kingdom of God, we need a notion of reconciliation or atonement centered on the cross.

There is a certain anti-authoritarian trend in contemporary theology that sees Christ's death on the cross as God's nonviolent way of subverting the powers that be (e.g., Weaver). In contrast to traditional Protestant conceptions of the atonement as a violent sacrifice to an angry God, this tradition says that we should speak of a nonviolent atonement where God does not inflict violence, but shows solidarity with our suffering in Christ. Those who defend the idea of a nonviolent atonement often point to early Christian theologians, who typically did not hold the later medieval and Protestant ideas of Christ's death as a violent sacrifice to God. Rather, as Gregory of Nyssa explained, Jesus' death was God's payment to death to buy and free humanity from the chains of the enemy. We have, by our sin ("the disease of love of rule," as Gregory puts it elsewhere) become the slaves of death. In our place, God overcomes the power of death through his powerlessness.[2] Jesus' death overcame the devil and the powers of death. God did not kill Jesus on the cross—humans did.

1. Origen, *On First Principles* 2, 5, 1–4.
2. Gregory of Nyssa, *Catechetical Discourse* 24, 1–4.

Contemporary theologians take this nonviolent idea of the atonement as a cue and explain that by his nonviolent approach to human evil, Jesus paved the way for a new kind of righteousness, where justice is not the product of retributive violence, but an alternative to violence. Sin is not overcome by vengeance, power, or domination, but by participating in the alternatives to sin and violence made possible by the cross. However, while there is an important point to the idea of a nonviolent atonement inspiring a new way of life, this is arguably only one perspective among others. The cross is *also* about God's judgment on sin. The cross is, as suggested above, God's final "No!" to all human unrighteousness (Barth)—the negation of all human attempts to become God by exercising judgment and power over one another. The cross is God's judgment on our judgments.

Jesus came in "the likeness of sinful flesh to be an atoning sacrifice," says Paul in his letter to the Romans (Rom 8:3). Although Jesus was without sin, he was "made sin" for us (2 Cor 5:21). That Jesus was without sin means that he did not attempt to gain power over others—as "sinful flesh" does. He was not subject to "the disease of love of rule," to reuse the phrase from Gregory of Nyssa. Jesus did not make himself God by judging others. But when Jesus took upon himself "the likeness of sinful flesh," it could be taken to mean that he took upon himself our identity as sinners who violently impose hierarchies of authority and domination upon one another. When God in Jesus condemns "sin in the flesh," as Paul puts it, this means that God in Jesus judges against all our attempts to become God by exercising power over each other.

The judgment of the cross, however, is more than just a judicial verdict. As early theologians such as Athanasius or Gregory of Nazianzus saw it, the whole of humanity mysteriously participated in Christ's death on the cross. We needed to die collectively in order to be freed from sin, but also to participate in the new creation realized in the resurrection: "We needed an incarnate and slain God in order to live," Gregory argued in an Easter sermon, adding: "We were killed with him so that we might be purified, and we were raised with him because we were killed with him."[3] Jesus was not just punished as a substitute for us, but humanity died with Christ on the cross: "One died for all, and therefore all died," says Paul (2 Cor 5:14). This has to do with the collective understanding of human nature that runs through biblical and much of early Christian theology. The classical idea of original sin should not be misunderstood to mean that sin is somehow "inherited" from one individual to the next. Modern individualism too often overlooks the biblical idea that we as individual persons share in a common humanity. It is this collective human nature, in which Christ was incarnated, that has "fallen" and been subjected to unrighteousness and sin.

All human persons participate in a common human nature. Original sin, or "the ancient transgression," as Athanasius called it, means that we are all in one way or another complicit in the unrighteousness that fundamentally ("originally" or "in principle") characterize the world as we know it. Unrighteousness, it may be argued, is about broken relations, which is why we don't become sinners individually, but always collectively. And just as we do not become sinners individually, we are not freed from sin individually. It is not only, for example, when we are baptized or come to faith, that we die "with Christ." We die with Christ already when humanity as such dies with him on the cross. Of course, we seem to be still very much alive, but our identity as people of unrighteousness, violence, and power has been crucified with Christ. Through the cross, humanity has been overcome.

Athanasius explained that Jesus had to die on a cross, and not, for example, of old age, because he had to die in public. Jesus had to die in the lowest, most humiliating way in order to reach all conditions of life. Jesus dies on the margins of society in order to include everyone in his reconciliation. As Athanasius so emphatically stated, "It is only on the cross that one dies with open arms."[4] While there are obviously other ways of dying with open arms, Athanasius's point was that Jesus dies with his arms open in order

3. Gregory of Nazianzus, *Oration* 45, 28.

4. Athanasius, *On the Incarnation* 25, 3.

to draw all people together and make them one. This was why Jesus could say, “When I am lifted up from the earth, I will draw all people to myself” (John 12:32), and why Christ can be said to bring peace, having broken down “the wall of partition” between Jews and gentiles in his body on the cross (Eph 2:14).

Still, this would not be very good news without a follow-up. We have died with Christ, all right, but then what? The loss of one’s identity is only good news if another, better identity is gained in its place. This is where the resurrection comes into the picture. Through the resurrection, a new humanity has been created, a reconciled humanity free from power and violence. All died in Christ in order that they should live with him, says Paul, adding that “if anyone is in Christ, the new creation has come: The old has gone, the new is here!” (2 Cor 5:15ff). From now on we regard “no one” according to “the flesh” or from a “worldly point of view,” as one translation puts it. That is, because our former identity has been crucified with Christ, we no longer perceive other people through the ideologies and structures of authority and domination that belong to “the flesh,” the present world order. Instead, we are to perceive ourselves and others through the new creation in Christ—the kingdom of God.

If the immanence of the kingdom is not understood with reference to the need for a new creation in Christ, it is flattened to a Romantic belief in the goodness of humanity. Instead, the kingdom of God is the kingdom of “the free and the freed” (Barth) who “reign in life” through Christ (Rom 5,17). Unrighteousness is a collective human condition, but all are made righteous in Christ, as Paul describes it in his letter to the Romans (Rom 5:18-19). Paul’s letter depicts a justice that can be equated with no political or religious order, but breaks in from the outside. This is why “justification by faith” is a matter of radical freedom. The kingdom of God is marked by the “law of independence and freedom” (Barth) secured by the new creation in Christ.

This is the background to Paul’s famous statement that “there is neither Jew nor Gentile, neither slave nor free, nor is there male and female, for you are all one in Christ Jesus” (Gal 3:28). In Christ there is no such thing as gender or ethnic identity, or identities defined by social or political orders, but all are one. The "lordship" of Christ is not a new kind of slavery, albeit of a more "universal" or benign kind, but a liberation from all kinds of slavery altogether. "It is for *freedom* that Christ has set us free," says Paul (Gal 5:1). For early Christian theologians, the new reality in Christ meant that such things as virtue and holiness could not consist in adherence to particular norms derived from, for example, gender. Of course men and women have differences, noted Clement of Alexandria, but the virtue of man and woman is the same: "There is one God of both, one Church—food, breath, sight, hearing, knowledge, hope, obedience, love are all the same."[5] In other words, as new creatures, we come to participate in Christ in whose image we were originally created. As Gregory of Nyssa argued, since humanity is created in the image of the infinite God, human nature eschews definition and comprehension.[6] Human identity in the kingdom of God transcends all categories of thought, all ideologies of culture, class, ethnicity, gender, and so on.

Of course, it seems that things are still very much subject to division, inequality, and injustice—it seems that our identity is still very much based on old ideologies. This is why we need faith to perceive our new identity in Christ. We need faith to "see" the invisible kingdom. Since our new identity cannot be "defined" through secular categories ("it has not yet been revealed what we shall be," 1 John 3:2), it takes faith to perceive it. At face value, we are still subject to injustice, relations of power, judgmentalism, political and religious ideology, and so on. But our true identity is not to be found in these things. Faith means coming to recognize that even though we can't *define* and *control* the new creation, it is nevertheless possible to follow Christ—by faith. In doing so it is possible to live a life that finds identity in the freedom and love of the kingdom. While we cannot escape the structures that are still present in the world, faith makes it possible to have hope for the new, resurrected life. For now, we are simultaneously the old

5. Clement of Alexandria, *The Instructor* 2, 8.

6. Gregory of Nyssa, *On the Making of Man* 155–56.

and the new creation—*simul peccator et justus*—subjects of both unrighteousness and the kingdom of God.

This is the distinction that Paul makes between "Adam" and "Christ" when he famously says, "As in Adam all die, so in Christ all will be made alive" (1 Cor 15:22). This will happen, says Paul, when Christ hands over the kingdom to his Father after having destroyed "all dominion, authority and power," and finally the power of death itself (1 Cor 15:20–28). Love will eventually replace power and domination. When Paul says that Christ will be subject to the Father, this should of course not be understood in terms of subordination. That would imply a dichotomy in the Trinity. Christ's subjection is a voluntary subjection in our place, resulting in a free participation in the life of God.

This was a crucial point made by fourth-century Christian theologians in defense of Trinitarian orthodoxy. Christ does not subject himself to God in his divine nature, since he has the same essence and will as the Father, which cannot, then, be subjected. But by subjecting his human body to God *for us*, he brings about the subjection of all humanity to God, argued Gregory of Nazianzus.[7] Subjection to God, argued Gregory of Nyssa, does not mean "servile submission," but God living "in us."[8] God, in other words, sets humanity free by finally abolishing all authority and power. The kingdom of God is not an external order imposed from above, but immanent in the most radical sense of being something intrinsic or "inner." It will *then* be correct to translate Jesus' famous words that the kingdom of God is "within you" and not just "in your midst" (Luke 17:21).

Salvation means a liberation from "servile submission" in a sense that is more than merely "spiritual." This becomes clear in Gregory of Nyssa's famous critique of slavery.[9] God does not make a slave of that which is free, he argued, but by his death and resurrection, Jesus has—in principle—freed humanity from all kinds of slavery once and for all. Not even God has the right to take away

7. Gregory of Nazianzus, *Oration* 30,5.

8. Gregory of Nyssa, *On the "Final Subjection" of Christ* 18.

9. Gregory of Nyssa, *Sermon on Ecclesiastes* 336.

human freedom, Gregory argued, since God's gifts are irrevocable (Rom 11:29). The death and resurrection of Christ frees humanity once and for all from identifying in terms of orders of domination. In other words, the gospel has direct implications for human freedom and equality in practice. Our death and resurrection with Christ makes the kingdom of God possible. But it also means that we must now live according to the new reality. Christian "ethics" is no longer about gaining access to the kingdom (even if theologians have often thought of it that way!), but a matter of behaving in a way that corresponds to our true identity in Christ.

V.

Principalities and Powers

For our struggle is not against flesh and blood, but against the rulers, against the authorities, against the powers of this dark world and against the spiritual forces of evil in the heavenly realms.

—EPHESIANS 6:12

THE universal significance of the gospel is constituted by the fact that God in Christ has reconciled the whole world to himself (2 Cor 5:19), thus rendering all worldly power, if not illegitimate, then at least at odds with the kingdom of God. Secular institutions may have a function, as long as the old and new creations coexist, but they will be limited, challenged, and ultimately dissolved by the kingdom of God. "Faith" does not mean the destructive demolition of secular institutions, but the awareness that "another world is possible." This awareness, however, may imply a conflict with powers that require human obedience by their claim to be absolute.

There is a cosmic perspective to the cross and the resurrection that is suggested by Paul's prophetic words on "dominion," "authority," and "power" (1 Cor 15:24). Paul also speaks of the "forces of the world" that enslaved us before Jesus redeemed us from the law (Gal 4:3). In principle, Christ has already disarmed the powers and authorities, having made "a public spectacle" of them by the cross (Col 2:15). There is still, however, an ongoing battle of cosmic proportions in which Christians are involved. This struggle is not against flesh and blood, but, as Paul saw it, against the rulers, authorities, and powers of "this dark world" and against "spiritual forces of evil in the heavenly realms" (Eph 6:12). There is obviously more to it than just "politics." The cross and the resurrection are about a cosmic struggle that involves the whole of creation (Rom 8:20). This does not mean that the cross has only a "spiritual" significance with no impact on social relations. It only means that the political significance of the cross has its source in a deeper spiritual context. Politics and spirituality are deeply interwoven in the Bible, not separated, as we are accustomed to thinking with a modern secularist worldview.

But what are the "principalities and powers," as older translations call them? Theologians have argued that the biblical worldview should be understood as "integral" in the sense that the visible and tangible are always closely interwoven with the spiritual (Wink). Only in the modern worldview do we make a sharp distinction between the "spiritual" and the "secular." The principalities and powers are the spiritual realities behind the secular order. In the premodern worldview, the principalities and powers were understood as spiritual realities, as fallen angels, for example. Sin has brought things out of balance, argued early theologians like Origen, but the restoration of creation to its original harmonious state will be the final result of Christ's atoning work. Today we might seek a more demythologized way of thinking of the principalities and powers. William Stringfellow argued that all organizations and institutions can in fact be understood biblically as principalities and powers. States and corporations are also powers in this sense. While not exactly reducing the spiritual to the material or sociological, the spiritual arguably cannot be entirely distinguished from it either. We encounter spiritual powers primarily through our encounters with secular powers—the power they exercise over us is rarely just physical, but psychological and spiritual as well.

If we follow Origen, the principalities and powers are the ontological realities behind particular moral and cultural norms. Every nation has its guardian angel, as described above. This is why there are differences, but also divisions and enmity, in the world. However, as Origen also explained, the kingdom of God is not governed by particular laws, but by the universal law of Christ. This is why the reconciliation of the world with God also leads to the reconciliation between peoples in the world. The cross breaks down the "wall of partition" between people (Eph 2:14), as it inaugurates a new community that is not divided by ethnic, religious, and political lines. Instead of adhering to moral norms posed by tradition and local customs, those who have their identity in the kingdom of God can now live by Christ's universal law of love and freedom. The struggle against the principalities and powers, then, is a matter of having an attitude of freedom toward secular customs and norms.

This understanding of the principalities and powers should be kept in mind when considering Paul's infamous teaching in Romans 13—even if here he is talking specifically of secular authorities. The authorities are "ordained" by God, but their purpose is temporary, and the church is not to participate in their ways or imitate their methods (Rom 12). We have already seen how early Christian theologians explained that Christians do not partake in military service, but this did not mean a complete hostility to secular powers. Origen explained that while Christians do not partake in upholding law and order by physical means, they offer their prayers to help the emperor preserve peace.[1] In other words, the early Christian denunciation of political power was not the same as saying that others (non-Christians), should not hold political office. The point is that while secular powers may be necessary in the world as it is, the church, whose identity is in the kingdom of God, should use alternative means in the struggle for justice and peace.

That early Christians prayed for the rulers—rather than against them—should remind us that the Christian attitude to

1. Origen, *Against Celsus* 8, 73.

politics cannot be a destructive, negative one. Resentment and an attitude of suspicion against the political elites, shared by some anti-establishment Christians today, too often replaces genuine concern for the public welfare. The struggle against the "powers" cannot be of a reactionary kind, if by "reaction" we understand returning evil for evil. Nor can it mean a complete withdrawal from the world. Rather, Christians are reminded of the positive possibility of acting with the love, forgiveness, and reconciliation of the kingdom that does not rely on domination and secular power (Eph 6:13–17). Positive ethics is the action that negates the form of this world (Barth). This positive "anarchic" approach may seem negative from the perspective of the principalities and powers. Not judging, not condemning, doing acts of love and mercy, may look like complicity with the chaos and disorder that the powers are supposed to keep in check through law and order. The struggle against the powers, however, must be a struggle to establish positive alternatives—not by force or violent means, whether of the physical or spiritual kind, but by "the gospel of peace" (Eph 6:15).

When Paul speaks about how Jesus will "destroy" all dominion, authority, and power (1 Cor 15:24), this could also be translated as "put down" or perhaps "level" or "subdue." Jesus' work is not destructive, but it transforms reality so that the principalities and powers are no longer forces of violence and domination, but become servants of love. This does not mean that the state or other institutionalized powers are "all right" if they just become "Christian." The state, it seems, cannot become fully Christian without ceasing to be the state. As the fourteenth-century Czech radical Petr Chelčický put it, when a king preaches instead of using force, he becomes a priest rather than a king. Of course, people may formally hold a position of authority without dominating others. This does not make their office "Christian," but an attitude of love formed by the gospel *is* possible even with formal positions of power.

As William Stringfellow suggested, the state and similar political powers are not the only principalities and powers out there. As mentioned in the above, "Mammon," money or wealth, is depicted in the New Testament as an idol or even a "god" that can easily take control of human life. To this degree, if we are not too rigid in our mythological definitions, wealth may also be counted among the principalities and powers. Economical rationality is the way of life, the ethics that accompanies the worship of wealth, when we obey Mammon. Capitalism, or the whole consumer *ethos* so prevalent in modern society, is a kind of religious practice. "Shopping" is an unholy substitute for the sacraments of the church.

There is a line of thought in biblical and early Christian theology that basically says that you become what you serve. Those who trust in idols become blind, numb, and senseless just like the idols (Ps 115). Greed—the idolatry of money—makes us cold-hearted and numb as we are trained in perceiving the world through economic rationality. To the naked eye, however, there is no such things as the "market" or the "economic system." Money has no objective value independent of the value that we project upon it. The principalities are spiritual powers, which means that they have power only to the degree that we trust or put faith in them. This does not mean that we can simply free ourselves from their power by an act of will, since they are collective realities that fundamentally shape our way of thinking. Only if something—the kingdom of God—breaks in from the outside, can the powers be broken.

For these reasons, twentieth-century "Christian anarchists" were often critical of capitalism with its economic rationality, but also of Marxism with its deterministic and materialist focus on production and labor. In many cases they were equally critical of technology. Jacques Ellul, for example, criticized technology (or *technique*), which he saw as humanity's attempt to dominate nature and humanity itself through rational methods. The danger of modern technology is that it has come to define the goal of all human action and behavior. New technologies are often presented as an extension of our freedom of choice, but it does not take long for new technologies to become mandatory and indispensable. For a time, we can delude ourselves into thinking that we are free to choose new technologies, but once they reach a certain level of adoption, we cannot avoid using them.

Technology becomes still more necessary for human interaction, defining how we relate to each other. As, for example, social media platforms come to hold a dominant position in how we develop our identity, technology also determines how we relate to ourselves and others. To this degree, technology has become a "power" that is easily at odds with the freedom that belongs to the kingdom of God. Technology connects people, but it also creates new occasions for division and polarization. It doesn't take much imagination to see the "slanderer" and buddies at work in online debates, conspiracy theories, cryptocurrencies, the dark web, and so on. Our addiction to social media is clear evidence of how technologies are not just neutral possibilities, but powers that seek to control our lives in every detail. Human relations are increasingly hyper-mediated through technology, regulated for profit, stifled and alienated. We need unmediated spaces for slow contemplation. Going to church, reading books, engaging in art, for example, without necessarily taking sides in upheaving conflicts, is an act of resistance against the powers of polarization and division.

There is still something to learn from Jacques Ellul's critical analysis of technology, which he saw as a totalitarian force that takes away human freedom. Efficiency had become a necessity that was imposed on all aspects of human life. Technology had even become "the unmoved mover," the all-determining "God" that requires religious obedience. Today, so-called "transhumanism" is an apt term for a technophile rebranding of the Nietzschean desire to "overcome" humanity—to create a new humanity through technological means, or even "build God" through artificial intelligence, as some say. Like all utopian idealism, such an effort overlooks the fact that a new humanity has already come into being in Christ, and that we already participate in it. To place our hopes in technology is not only idolatry, but a denial of the reality of the kingdom.

The almost fatalistic view of technology, however, may not quite fit the experience of postmodern life. It is true, as Ellul observed, that technology is constantly accelerating, always moving toward greater efficiency and the growth of possibilities. It seems, however, that there is also a countercurrent built into technology itself. We tend to push the capacity of new technologies to the limit—and beyond. This results in gaps and glitches that keep appearing even as technology continues to be improved. This is how we get, for example, the "non-space," classically exemplified by the airport. Flying is the quickest and most efficient form of transportation. However, the time we have to wait at the airport is an example of how technology, for all its efficiency, often leaves us hanging in gaps of time and space—quite literally. Perhaps this is something to be celebrated as an opportunity for freedom. The "non-space" is an "apophatic" space, a space that lacks a clear purpose or meaning. To this degree, technology, by its very lack, inadvertently cracks open the conditions for alternative modes of being.

In other words, the principalities and powers often fall short in their attempts to control human life. This makes it possible to search for the gaps in the seemingly totalitarian conditions of postmodern life. Not necessarily with the aim of "filling" the gaps, but perhaps rather to keep open the "non-spaces" that we encounter. We need spaces for reflection and meditation in the classical Christian sense of freely pondering on spiritual matters without necessarily having to perform or produce anything or go anywhere. The opportunities to point to the kingdom of God do not so much exist in alternative *systems*, but may be found in the narrow cracks and spaces of freedom that appear at the margins of the systems themselves.

Like the principalities and powers, "demons" are mythological creatures that play a role in the story of salvation. Origen explained that according to God's law, the "demons" mentioned in the New Testament had originally no right to rule over the earth.[2] They were nevertheless allowed to rule over people who had chosen to submit to evil—until Christ came to set people free. In the traditional, premodern worldview, demons are spiritual entities that can somehow "move in" and live in a person as in a house. While not necessarily discarding such notions altogether, being "possessed" may equally mean to be entangled in the spiritual

2. Origen, *Against Celsus* 8, 33–34.

structures that surround us. The internal and the external are not easily distinguished. Rather, it is the demonic powers that bind us to the spiritual powers that shape social, religious, cultural, and economic relations among people. When Jesus casts out demons, he is not simply freeing people from their individual sickness and symptoms, but he sets people free from the structures of sin, oppression, and injustice that permeate the present world order.

These were points emphasized by the "social gospel." The church has done much over the years to focus on individual sin, Walter Rauschenbusch noted, but it has forgotten to address the sin that characterizes the institutions and structures in society. The gospel is about the kingdom of God, not just the private salvation of the individual. As such it is also about a new social order that is fundamentally different from the one we are accustomed to. Jesus not only liberates people from their bondage to the *cosmos*, but salvation means being transferred to a new kingdom. Jesus warns that seven new spirits will move into the house that has been cleansed (Matt 12:44–45). This should remind us that it is not possible to live as a "free" individual with no spiritual ties. True freedom is only possible when the Holy Spirit binds us to the kingdom of God.

From a more ontological point of view, we may argue that the principalities and powers are not really "beings," at least not to the degree that they are forces of evil. In classical Christian theology from the third century and onward, evil was in philosophical terms seen as the privation of good, not something that had a substantial being of its own. This is, in a sense, the "banality" of evil (Arendt). God was often called *omnipotent* or *almighty*, but this should not be taken to mean that God determines every detail in world history, both good and evil. Christian theologians agreed that God is not the cause of evil, but evil occurs when the harmony of creation is broken because of sin.

The power of evil is really "the power of nothingness" (Barth). This is again why the struggle of Christians against the "powers," should not be considered *destructive*, but rather as radically *constructive*. We cannot solve "the problem of evil," but we can do what we can to mitigate evil with good—instead of trying to overcome evil with evil (Rom 12:21). Fighting the powers is not about tearing things down, but about identifying broken relations or the absence of love, and prayerfully doing what you can to restore what has been lost and broken.

VI.

What Is the Church?

We are therefore Christ's ambassadors, as though God were making his appeal through us. We implore you on Christ's behalf: Be reconciled to God.

—2 CORINTHIANS 5:20–21

SEEKING the kingdom should not be confused with self-marginalization or polarizing attitudes toward politics and culture. The *ethos* that follows from the concept of the kingdom of God as "anarchy" cannot be directly translated into secular politics. If we can speak of a "Christian anarchism" at all, it must be primarily an ecclesiological concept—a matter of understanding what it means for the church to be shaped by the kingdom regardless of its attitude to the "world." While the kingdom of God is not something that can be organized by human means, the church should reflect the kingdom of God in its way of being in the world.

Gregory of Nyssa argued that the church is the new "world" or "order" that Paul mentioned in his epistle to the Romans.[1] The "invisible things of God" that have been clearly perceived since the foundation of the world (Rom 1:20) are not God's ineffable being, but the economy of salvation that is proclaimed by the church in word and practice. The economy of salvation revealed through

1. Gregory of Nyssa, *On the Song of Songs* 384–86.

the church is God's "manifold wisdom" (Eph 3:10) by which the power of the enemy is overcome through the powerlessness of the cross. Through the church, says Gregory, it is revealed how God has fashioned a new humanity born "from above" after the image of God. This new humanity, Gregory adds, reflects the God who is becoming "all in all" (1 Cor 15:28).

As such, the church can hardly be pitted against the rest of humanity. The church is that particular place where the whole of humanity is revealed as in the process of being restored by Christ. The church is where it becomes possible to identify with the "new humanity," the "anarchic" community that is free from power and domination through its participation in the life and love of Christ and the kingdom of God. This identification should not be confused with a sectarian belief that the church somehow possesses the kingdom of God. Nor should it lead to an attempt to fit people into a particular "Christian" subculture. As a message of freedom and love, the gospel of the kingdom runs counter to all domination and authoritarianism, both in politics and religion.

Considered as *ekklesia,* the church is literally the "called-out" people of God. The church gathers not to talk, but to listen—and to give others the opportunity to join in on listening. The church is not a private club, but a public assembly. Privacy is against its very nature. It is, however, easy to miss this point when studying the history of the church. When the early Christians were forced into hiding by persecution, they naturally took on the character of an "esoteric" society. Today, in countries where Christians are persecuted, this may be the only possible strategy for survival. This does not mean, however, that the "house church," for example, is closer to the heart of the gospel or an absolute ideal to be followed for all time. As soon as the persecutions ceased in antiquity, the church re-entered the public sphere.

The solution to a perceived crisis in secular society cannot be an exile from "mainstream culture" in order to construct a "Christian counterculture," as some theologians suggest from time to time. The freedom of the kingdom means that there can be no such thing as a neatly defined, peculiar "Christian morality" or Christian "ethics." The kingdom operates at a deeper level than what can be codified in a set of moral norms. This means that being church cannot be about creating subcultures or societies within society with their own peculiar codes of conduct. It is not the job of the church to make society conform to this or that "Christian moral order," as if there could be such a thing, but to point to what God has already done for the world in Christ—so that society may be permeated and transformed from within by the love and freedom that flow from the kingdom.

Does this mean that the kingdom of God is only a matter of private piety and not real politics—of "changing hearts rather than laws," for example—after all? Far from it. Even if the kingdom cannot be translated into this or that political ideology, as we learn to appreciate humility, love, and mercy rather than power and wealth, this will surely affect our approach to politics. This should not, however, take the form of a judgmental attitude to secular politics. The church cannot weaponize the kingdom and require that the state conform to it by, for example, giving up its call to defend law and order. In a "politics of peace," Vernard Eller observed, "we have no right to call a secular state to become defenseless." We should first ask what *we* can do to promote peace. When addressing the contemporary political situation, the church can only ask itself whether it has been successful in pointing to the God who has become humble for our sake.

The church is a public witness to the kingdom of God, not a sect hiding from the open. The church is the ambassador of the word of reconciliation, as Paul describes the apostolic vocation (2 Cor 5:20). The church can be this only to the degree that it first finds itself in a position of humility and an attitude of openness to the kingdom of God. The church consists of whoever hears the message of the kingdom. It does not possess the gospel as an instrument or a weapon to be wielded in political battles or culture wars—whether from a "progressive" or "conservative" standpoint. As argued by dialectical theology, the gospel places the church in solidarity with the world under the judgment of God's mercy (e.g., Rom 11:32). This calls into question whatever we do to control things. The response can be activity where there is passivity and passivity where things are getting too busy, but it can never mean simply doing the opposite of what the "world" does. The kingdom transcends all binary opposites. Reconciliation must be the goal of all critique.

Since God has already reconciled the world to himself, the job of the church is not to build or realize the kingdom of God, as if it were an ideal to be put into practice. The job of the church is to call people to become aware of their reconciliation in Christ. As Baptist preacher and author Will Campbell put it, in a sense, we are to do "nothing." We are to stop pretending that reconciliation is something we must bring about through the exercise of political and organizational power. Reconciliation means letting go of our feeble attempts to realize the kingdom of God, as if we had not already been reconciled to God through Christ.

That we should do "nothing" in this sense does not, however, mean that we do not need the church. We cannot make do with an individualistic idea of "Christian anarchism" as opposed to all forms of order in society and church. The dialectical idea of the kingdom of God as the antithesis of all secular order should not be confused for a negative dualism with no room for God's ongoing atoning work in the world. The church not only bears witness to the incomprehensible kingdom, but also participates in the work of God through the Holy Spirit. The kingdom reveals itself not only in opposition to the world, but also through human language, culture, and—perhaps—even politics. But in doing so, it transforms language, culture, and politics from within. The result is that secular politics, which is really only a parody of the church's "true politics" (Cavanaugh), is transformed.

The true politics of the church consists in the sacramental participation in Christ. Secular politics can at best approximate the kingdom by analogy. The "being" of the church is a participation in the kingdom of God, and as such true "anarchic" politics. The church is not just one organization among others dedicated to communicating certain Christian doctrines to people. The gospel is not just a collection of propositions about sin and salvation that individuals can choose to intellectually assent to. The gospel is the symbolic narration of the kingdom in ever new forms. The church is by its participation the embodiment of this message. The church is to *be* the gospel—not, of course, the good news about the church itself, but the good news about the kingdom. For this reason, the "form" of the church cannot be separated from the "form" of the gospel.

This is why the relations among the disciples are so important in the teachings of Jesus. The disciples are to be "one" so the world may believe (John 17:21–24)—the church should invite people into its participation in the unity of God. As mentioned in the above, Clement of Alexandria described the church as the community of those who participate in the common *logos*.[2] This community anticipates the universal community that all people will eventually partake of. The church, it could be added, is not in "opposition" to the world, which is being transformed by God. The church is in opposition to the world only to the extent that the world stubbornly rejects its reconciled identity in Christ. In other words, the opposition is asymmetrical: the church is not opposed to the world even if the world may be opposed to the church—in a sense there is nothing to *be* opposed to, as the world is in principle already dissolved by the cross and reestablished by the resurrection of Christ.

Perhaps most crucial to understanding the form of the church is Jesus' exhortation to his disciples about not dominating one another as do "the rulers" and "the high officials of the gentiles" (Matt 20:25–28). "Not so with you," says Jesus. This is not only a criticism of worldly power politics. It is also a positive description of how things should be in the church: "Whoever wants to become great *among you* must be your servant," says Jesus (Matt 20:26). The relations among the disciples are not mediated through "representation," but is a matter of equal *participation* in God through Christ. As such, Jesus' words about serving rather than ruling have immense consequences for how we understand "service" and "leadership" in a Christian context. Jesus is not just making a point

2. Clement of Alexandria, *The Instructor* 2, 12, 120.

about what it means for individuals to imitate him, but he is giving an account of how relations look like in a church marked by the presence of the kingdom of God.

Perhaps we can even understand Jesus' words about serving rather than ruling as "the constitution of the church," as the nineteenth-century Danish-German Baptist pioneer Julius Köbner did: "Domination, power and coercion are against the essence of Christianity," he argued in his *Manifesto* shortly after Karl Marx in 1848. The "politics" of the Christian is the kingdom of God, Köbner also argued. For Baptists like Köbner, for the church to imitate Jesus meant that the congregation should make all decisions through democratic voting. Perhaps today a form of deliberative democracy or consensus decision-making—as modeled, for example, by Quakers—could inspire as an alternative to how the "great" rule their people.

The kingdom of God should not, however, be confused with a specific church order. Neither can we simply take over theories of leadership and decision-making from, for example, political philosophy. Such theories too easily risk becoming empty idols that may look very similar to the kingdom of God, but are nevertheless devoid of the love and freedom that belong to the kingdom. We cannot induce love and freedom through rules of conduct, even if such rules are helpful or even necessary in practice. Nor can we borrow models of leadership from the business world and apply them in a church setting, as is popular in some churches. There is a vast amount of literature and conferences on "leadership" in and outside the church. The kingdom, however, does not lend itself to such ambitions. Instead, we must take our cue from Jesus himself. We need to reflect on what he might have meant when he said that we are not to rule over one another, and that we are not to call ourselves "master," "teacher" or "father" (Matt 23:8). This does not mean that there cannot be so-called "leadership" or offices in the church, but it does mean that our understanding and attitude to such offices should be quite different from what we know from other contexts.

Paul may not seem to have followed Jesus in his anti-authoritarian description of the church. For example, Paul can say that wives are to obey their husbands and that slaves are to obey their masters, and so on (Eph 6:6–9 and Eph 5:21–25). Importantly, however, Paul also makes it clear that husbands should serve their wives, and that the slave owner should treat his slave as a brother. To this degree, he does in fact seem to follow Jesus' words about how the powerful should become servants. Paul, it can be argued, is sensitive to the gradual and organic way in which the kingdom grows. The egalitarianism of the gospel does not necessarily overturn or replace cultural and societal norms all at once, but it gradually transforms them from within. In doing so, it renders them superfluous by dissolving the hierarchical thinking that feeds them. This may prove to be much more efficient than simply trying to replace one set of moral norms with another. It may take more time and work than a sudden, violent revolution—and it has often been used as an excuse for perpetuating inequality. The kingdom, however, subverts and transforms structures slowly but more efficiently than any violent political revolution.

While some degree of authoritarianism crept into the church from early on, skepticism about leadership was prevalent among early Christians. For example, they often had a hard time finding people who were willing to lead as bishops. Origen explained, in his apology against Celsus, that "we do not accept those who love power," but call those who are competent to take office. Origen even argued that "those who rule us well are those who have had to be forced to take office."[3] Obviously we cannot force people to become pastors or bishops, but this line of thinking should remind us that a reluctant attitude toward leadership was considered a virtue by many early Christians—just think of the fourth-century saint Martin of Tours, who hid himself among the geese when his fellow Christians wanted to ordain him as a bishop. Martin, a former soldier, is said to have been a pacifist ("I am a soldier of Christ now, it is not lawful for me to fight"), and he certainly seems

3. Origen, *Against Celsus* 8, 75.

to have had no ambitions of leadership—which was at least one reason why he was fit to become a bishop.

Such skeptical attitudes toward leadership do not mean that, for example, a Free Church or a democratic Baptist ecclesiology is necessarily more to the point than the organized structures of traditional mainline churches. The Danish Lutheran Church, which has the majority of the population as its members, is a good example of how a well-established church supported and to some extent even governed by the state can in fact be more open and inclusive than many small independent congregations with only local leadership. The state can actually help keep the church avoid sectarianism and hierarchical models by checking the ambitions of those eager to "lead." The Catholic Workers are also an example of how "Christian anarchism" may actually thrive in large ecclesiastical organizations with hierarchical leadership, as long as this gives room for alternative modes of being. Living according to Jesus' exhortation to serve rather than to rule may not depend so much on external structures, though it cannot be reduced to something purely "inner" or "spiritual" either.

There is also a point to be made about ecumenical relations among the churches. The "unity" or "oneness" of the church ("that they all may be one," John 17:23) is not a distinctive *quality* of the church. The oneness of the church can be understood dialectically as the absence of any distinctive qualities that, when made absolute, can become the cause of division. Divisions between churches arise when we make absolute claims to have the right theology, ethics, liturgy, order, and so on. The work for ecumenical unity among the churches cannot, however, be a matter of creating a unity that does not yet exist. "Ecumenism" is not only constructive, but must also consist in breaking down the walls of partition that jeopardize the unity that in principle is already there. The oneness of the church consists in its poverty—its lack of qualities—which means that its unity can only come from God. This understanding should also shape how the church relates to the world and people in which it is situated. The church does not "possess" something that the world "needs," but it can only point—in word and practice—to what we all need.

The church should be a place where people come together in a common prayer that God may have "mercy upon all" (Rom 11:32). Christians do not just pray for themselves, but for the world. As Karl Barth famously put it, "to clasp the hands in prayer is the beginning of an uprising against the disorder of the world." The Lord's Prayer is not just about individual piety, even if it is to be prayed in "the unseen" (Matt 6:6), but an act of solidarity *with* and *for* the world. Prayer is not personal, argued William Stringfellow, in the sense of being a private, disconnected transaction. Prayer is a political act, bridging the gap between the world as it is and the kingdom to come.

Although the exhortation to "preach the gospel, if necessary using words" is often misattributed to Francis of Assisi, the saying contains the obvious truth that the gospel is *also* a matter of practice. The gospel is "spiritual," all right, but spiritual does not mean private or abstract. In practice, the Holy Spirit is present in works of love and charity. Loving one's neighbor is what it means to be a "practicing" Christian. A healthy Protestant skepticism about works righteousness should not deter the church from engaging in diaconal work in its daily life. When James notes that true religion is to care for orphans and widows (Jas 1:27), this should not simply be discarded as Judaic legalism. The righteousness of Christ, in which the church participates, shapes not only the faith of its individual members, but also its corporate social work.

This idea is present in many early Christian writings, for example the *Epistle to Diognetus*. Here the clear belief in how God works through persuasion and kindness, rather than violence and coercion, was connected to the idea that Christians do not pursue riches and power, but instead help those in need. Christians are "citizens of heaven," but at face value they exhibit no peculiar way of life.[4] Christians seem invisible in society, since they do not observe any particular religious customs, the epistle argues, but they are nevertheless characterized by their love for neighbors.

4. *Epistle to Diognetus* 5, 4.

Christians do not pursue money and power, but love others like Christ has done. Imitating God is incompatible with violence and domination, but the strong can imitate God by helping the weak.[5]

Thus, *diakonia*—literally "serving"—is an indispensable part of the gospel as expressed in the life of the church. As progressives often assert, the church should be a place where sinners, outsiders, and the marginalized can find rest, not an exclusive club for the holier-than-thou: Like Jesus, the church should attract those in need, even at the risk of repelling the religiously self-righteous. This, of course, is easier said than done. Jesus attracted sinners because he was capable of sharing the kingdom without suffering loss or making others instruments of his own righteousness. The classical notion of the "impassibility" of God suggests that God can give to the world without becoming "less" in doing so. The church, however, consists of ordinary people who do not have unlimited resources of love to share. This, however, is only one more reason why *diakonia* should be a matter of solidarity rather than of distanced generosity.

It is of course well-intentioned when we say with Bonhoeffer that the church is only church when it exists for others. There is the danger, however, that in doing so we make a distinction between the church and "the others," which is not true solidarity. Of course, it can be argued that the New Testament does distinguish between "the church" and "the world," but this distinction is immediately dissolved in relation to God. That the kingdom of God is not "of this world" (John 18:36) means that the church must be present *in* and *with* the world, as the place where it becomes possible *for* the world to hear about its reconciliation with God and the presence of the kingdom.

The church must not, then, become a place where the spiritually and materially "well off" serve the "others" in "need." If it does, it perpetuates the distinction between insiders and outsiders dissolved by the gospel. Our neighbor is not a means we can use in making ourselves good people. The church should be a place where we recognize humanity's common brokenness and need for

5. *Epistle to Diognetus* 10, 4–5.

God, thereby dissolving all ideas of the "inside." It is true that the church should be a place of "radical inclusion," as it is sometimes argued, but perhaps it is even more accurate to say that the church should be a place of "radical exclusion"—if by that phrase we mean a place where all people can take part in the kingdom of God as outsiders and marginalized. This means transcending all cultural, social, and political categories and focusing instead on our identity in Christ.

The key to this, perhaps surprisingly, may be to maintain a liturgical awareness and even a certain kind of traditionalism. The progressivist urge for a church that is constantly "moving forwards" can be just as violent as the reactionary opposition to any change. The church should not forget its unique identity as a witness to the kingdom of God. Liturgy remains necessary for the church to maintain its awareness of the kingdom, even if the Christianity that has "come of age" should move away from religion and focus on prayer and work for justice (Bonhoeffer). While early sources such as the *Epistle to Diognetus* made the claim mentioned above, that Christians had no special religious practice—except the negative one of not worshiping idols, power, and wealth—it could be argued today that we need religious practices exactly to remind us of the radical otherness of the kingdom.

The modern antipathy to organized religion sometimes leads to a forgetfulness of the theological basis of the church's social engagement. What distinguishes the church from many secular humanitarian organizations is that the church's social work is rooted not in abstract ideals, but in the kingdom of God and the concern for the neighbor in the concrete person. To make this clear we need liturgy, that is, we need rituals, art, music, and an organized way of meeting. Although the kingdom is not a matter of religion, it can express itself even through religion. The church should practice a liturgical culture that is not ruled by secular demands for efficiency and productivity, but serves as a witness to the kingdom of God. The church must be shaped by the gospel, and so must its practices, including the entire liturgy.

Liturgy, defined as "the service of the people," has a political significance. Originally, it referred to the sacrificial cult of pagan religion. However, when the church celebrates the sacrifice of Christ, the political meaning of liturgy is transformed. It becomes a testimony that God has overcome powers and authorities. It serves as a witness to the immanence of the kingdom of God. The liturgy is in a sense "pointless" because it testifies to the kingdom of God—the "eternal Sabbath rest"—that exists only for its own sake, and has no instrumental purpose beyond itself. The liturgy is not a means for establishing the kingdom, but a sign of its presence. Sacraments or ordinances such as baptism and the Lord's Supper are the gospel in visible and tangible form. Baptism, as Walter Rauschenbusch noted, was originally not just a ritual for the salvation of the individual, but an incorporation into a religious-social movement with the kingdom of God as its goal. In baptism, we receive an identity that is not subject to spiritual or secular powers, political ideologies, social roles, or culture. Baptism is ultimately a political act that anticipates the future when Christ will subdue all power and authority so that God can become "all in all" (1 Cor 15:28).

Although the church has always seen baptism as a requirement for membership, it should be considered a free gift and not as a means of control. The freedom that pertains to the kingdom should shape how we understand and practice baptism—whether it is of children or as credo-baptism—as well as the Lord's Supper. As Jürgen Moltmann noted, the truly evangelical character of the Lord's Supper is destroyed if it is limited by hierarchical, dogmatic, and moral legalism. The Lord's Supper testifies to the unity of the kingdom of God. Like baptism, it is essentially a political act, as it bears witness to the victory over the powers and authorities that Jesus realized on the cross. The Lord's Supper testifies that another world, defined not by power but love, is possible. This is arguably why Paul emphasized that his readers in Corinth should think twice before partaking in the Lord's Supper (1 Cor 11:28). The point is not so much to contemplate individual sins, but to make sure that the common meal really does express the mutuality and love of which it is a sign.

In general, liturgy should reflect the well-ordered anarchy of the kingdom. For example, communal singing in the church should not be led by a "worship leader," but only backed up if needed. Leadership in the church must always be conceived of as service. This of course makes large gatherings impractical, but if the church is not about power and size, this may not be so bad after all. Rightly perceived, liturgy is not empty religious rituals or entertainment, but a living participation in the kingdom of God. This participation must find its ultimate expression not in the rituals themselves, but in the love and freedom made possible by the presence of the kingdom.

VII.

Hope for All

Then the end will come, when he hands over the kingdom to God the Father after he has destroyed all dominion, authority and power. For he must reign until he has put all his enemies under his feet. The last enemy to be destroyed is death. For he "has put everything under his feet." Now when it says that "everything" has been put under him, it is clear that this does not include God himself, who put everything under Christ. When he has done this, then the Son himself will be made subject to him who put everything under him, so that God may be all in all.

—1 CORINTHIANS 15:24-28

ONE thing that may seem puzzling at first sight is that people who identify—or at least are identified by others—as "Christian anarchists" also tend to believe that all humans will eventually be saved. A critical attitude to power and domination seems to be linked to some sort of soteriological universalism. Digging deeper for the reasons grounding both beliefs makes it clear that the two are intimately related. This is true even if by no means all Christian universalists can be described as "anarchists." However, the anti-authoritarian view of God, politics, and the church fits well with an inclusive and hopeful attitude toward people and creation in general—if the kingdom breaks down all barriers and distinctions, it seems fair to conclude that God is in fact "the savior of all" (1 Tim 4:10).

The belief in "the restoration of all things," the *apokatastasis pantôn* in Greek, was widespread in the early church, at least since Origen in the third century. Origen based his belief that all rational beings would eventually be saved on Paul's words, quoted above, about how God would eventually become "all in all" when all authorities had been subdued by Christ (1 Cor 15:20–28). Paul saw this as realized gradually. The resurrection of all with Christ is first made possible by Christ's own resurrection. Then comes the resurrection of those "who belong to him." Finally, the goal is reached when all dominion, authority, and power is subjected to Christ so that God can become "all in all" (1 Cor 15:28). This was also the point when John's first epistle could say that Christ is "the atoning sacrifice for our sins, and not only for ours but also for the sins of the whole world" (1 John 2:2). The point was, says Origen, that Jesus is not only the atoning sacrifice for the faithful, but for the whole world, although in that specific order.[1] The power of the cross of Christ is so strong that it heals and restores "not only the present," but also "future and past times." It reaches not only to "the human order," but also to "heavenly powers and orders."[2] The subjugation of the powers is really their conversion and restoration to harmony.

This line of thought was echoed in the fourth century, when theologians like Gregory of Nyssa and his sister Macrina saw the hope of a universal salvation as closely connected to a belief in the unity of human nature. We have already seen that for Gregory of Nyssa, the critique of power and domination had to do with the fact that human relations are meant to reflect the equal relations of the Trinitarian God. All humans, created in the image of God, share a common human nature. This makes divisions among humans contrary to nature. The unity of human nature also means that salvation is not just something individual. Salvation means a restoration (or the final realization) of the unity of

1. Origen, *Commentary on Romans* 3, 8.

2. Origen, *Commentary on Romans* 5, 10.

human nature—which, of course, can only happen if all humans are ultimately saved.

The freedom of the creature is achieved by the termination of its bondage, argued Origen. This is fulfilled when Christ delivers up his kingdom to the Father so that God can become "all in all."[3] Gregory of Nyssa, commenting on Paul's words in 1 Corinthians, made it clear that submission to God is not something involuntary and coerced, but a free submission that is really a union in the love of God.[4] It means being united to God by participating in God's freedom rather than being subjected to a hierarchy of power. Though we may have to go through long periods of purification, eventually, argued Gregory, no created being will fall outside the boundaries of the kingdom of God.[5] Similarly, Macrina argued that the "fire" that punishes sinners should be seen as purifying. The fire is the judgment that God uses to purify us from everything that keeps us from participating in the freedom and love of God. It may literally take ages (*aions* in Greek), but eventually God will be "all in all"—which for Macrina, as mentioned above, was another way of saying that humanity had become self-governing and autonomous by participating in God's freedom.[6]

As theologians have often pointed out, "eternal" in the Bible does not necessarily mean "everlasting" in a temporal sense. It can also mean the span of an age, or the special quality of what comes from the eternal God, as in "eternal life" in the present. Only the kingdom is eternal in the absolute sense, but God's judgments are historical and temporary, having salvation—the restoration of justice—as their goal. For example, as Paul explains, Israel is only temporarily (and only seemingly) rejected so that the gospel can be brought to the gentiles. When "the full number of the Gentiles has come in" (presumably in the kingdom of God), then "all Israel will be saved" (Rom 11:25–26). The whole point of such

3. Origen, *On First Principles* 1, 7, 5.

4. Gregory of Nyssa, *On the "Final Subjection" of Christ* 18.

5. Gregory of Nyssa, *On the "Final Subjection" of Christ* 8.

6. Macrina according to Gregory of Nyssa, *On the Soul and the Resurrection* 100–104.

historical dialectics is to make it clear that humans cannot be saved by their own efforts, but only by grace: "God has bound everyone over to disobedience so that he may have mercy on them all," says Paul (Rom 11:32). This, it seems, is how God turns that which is "something" in the eyes of the world into "nothing" (1 Cor 1:28), but only in order to level and finally dissolve all human claims to power. The purpose is not the final destruction of anyone, but to make it clear that no act of will makes anyone capable of mastering the kingdom of God. The kingdom comes by grace, contrary to all human achievements and claims to power.

Paul's theology, as Jacob Taubes argued, is polemical not only against the Jewish law, but also against the Roman Empire or any authoritarian conception of politics that runs counter to the kingdom of God. The destruction (or deconstruction, we might say) of power structures is central to the cosmological battle between Christ and the powers. In parallel, modern political utopias—for example the classless society—has often been seen as secularized versions of the Christian hope in the "restoration of all things." The difference, of course, is that the secular versions of this hope has is many cases been based on optimistic or even naive beliefs in humanity's ability to create paradise on earth—often by force and violence. Such impossible efforts frequently disappoint. The gospel, however, is about the possibility that belong to God alone: the kingdom that is impossible for us, but in principle already achieved by Christ. Salvation is not an ideal that we need to realize, but a reality always already at work in the world.

Some Reformed theologians, like Jeremiah White in the seventeenth century and Jacques Ellul in the twentieth, went so far as to argue that all people are in principle saved "from eternity" (in the sense of having been saved already before creation through the election of humanity in Christ). The church is no different from others in this respect, although it does have a specific role to play as the ambassadors of God here and now. The church are the elect who gather in attendance to the fact that they—like the rest of the world (2 Cor 5:19)—have been reconciled to God through Christ. The church is called to anticipate the kingdom of God, where all hierarchies and divisions among people are dissolved. In this sense there is a distinction between those who are "being saved" and those who are "perishing" (1 Cor 1:18). This distinction cannot, however, be considered absolute or ultimate. The only real distinction in which we all participate is—understood dialectically—the distinction between the unrighteous humanity that is perishing, and the new creation in Christ that is being saved: "For as in Adam all die, so in Christ all will be made alive" (1 Cor 15:22).

This conception of eschatology impacts how the church proclaims the gospel. The gospel cannot be preached by manipulation or forced upon people. Paul notes that when he first preached the gospel in Corinth, he did so with meekness rather than with clever rhetoric and the power of worldly wisdom. This means that, for example, apologetics cannot be a matter of winning arguments. Apologetics must be a matter of gently telling stories of faith and love in practice, rather than violently manipulating people. As the Danish pastor-theologian K. Olesen Larsen once argued, "The gospel wants only servants, not guardians and rulers; the gospel loses all that people gain in power." Of course, as mentioned above, the New Testament also contains the idea that the church is engaged in a spiritual battle. However, this battle is not against people, but the church fights "intellectual strongholds" that set themselves up against the knowledge of God (2 Cor 10:5). Just as Jesus fought the powers by becoming powerless, so this battle is fought not with aggression or power, but with love, patience, compassion, peace, and prayer.

In the apocalypse of John, Christ fights the powers with the word that comes out of his mouth depicted as a sword (Rev 19:15). This is, of course, to be read with the gospel as the hermeneutical key. The apocalypse is only *prima facie* about Jesus coming back with a "commitment to make someone bleed." As theologians have argued, if there's blood, it's Christ's own (Boyd). Jesus' divine character of self-sacrificial love does not change. Just as before, he fights the powers by serving, and the church should do the same. It may be necessary, of course, to bluntly criticize false conceptions of the gospel that make God into a violent or authoritarian despot.

Even John the Baptist, who was anything but timid in pronouncing judgment on the Pharisees and others, does not hesitate to quote Isaiah's saying that "all people will see God's salvation" (Luke 3,6). The job of the church is not to condemn, but to pray for all, simply because it is the will of God that all people are saved (1 Tim 2:1–7). As Christoph Blumhardt reminds us, if we should give up hope for any person or nation, Jesus would not be the one who holds the universe together—and his cross would not be a cosmic cross that brings everything back together.

"Let the Cross of Christ be the banner under which we fight," wrote the nineteenth-century English Baptist minister Samuel Cox, adding, "Let us maintain that the Atonement made by Him, as it was intended for all, so also must it extend to all." Perhaps we do not need such soteriological universalism in order to appreciate the "anarchist" perspective on the kingdom of God. Of course, there are other ways of reading the New Testament. Nevertheless, the gospel seems to be at its most radical when it is understood to be about a kingdom that does away with all hierarchies and distinctions between people. The goal is that everything will be subject to God when all dominion, authority, and power are nullified and abolished. Then God will be "all in all."

Afterword

Negative Political Theology?

It may be argued that the above hardly amounts to more than a "democratic" idea, although perhaps a radical one, but not "anarchy." Nicolai Berdyaev argued, as mentioned in the introduction, that as a political idea anarchism is both naive and destructive, but he added that true democracy may vaguely reflect the anarchy of the kingdom of God.[7] It may also be argued that classical Trinitarian theology does not allow for the notion of the kingdom of God as "anarchy" in the strict sense. After all, isn't God the Father the only one who is *anarchos,* without beginning? The "monarchy" of the Father in classical Trinitarian thought means that the Father is the origin of the Son and the kingdom, which cannot, it seems, be considered without origin or as "anarchy." Perhaps, the kingdom should rather be seen as a "monarchy," which is, after all, just another word for a kingdom.

These objections may be true to some degree, but they do not capture the deeply apophatic intuitions at play in the original claim that the kingdom of God is anarchy. The kingdom of God is—to put it in paradoxical terms—a well-ordered anarchy. Rather than being defined as this or that particular order of things, it must be present as a line of negation through whatever concepts of order that we may hold. The "monarchian" notion of God the Father as the beginning without beginning, or the ruler without rule, must be paired with the Trinitarian notion of the anarchic,

7. Berdyaev, *Slavery and Freedom,* 148.

beginning-less, birth of the Son.[8] The Son is the kingdom itself, as argued by Origen, or perhaps, as Gregory of Nazianzus saw it, the Trinity is the kingdom itself—a kingdom that is, at any rate, free of subordination and domination.[9] Gregory equated "polyarchy" with "brawling anarchy," as both were equally far from the "strong-shining Monarchy" of the Trinity.[10] The unity of Father, Son, and Holy Spirit means, however, that they cannot be divided in power or will, which is why they are one harmonious whole. To participate in God must, then, mean to participate in a kingdom in which there are no relations of domination and subordination. The kingdom of God is an "anarchic monarchy," so to speak, in which humanity is called to participate. Submission to God means paradoxically, as Gregory of Nyssa and Macrina argued, to participate in the freedom of God. Participation in the kingdom means participating in an order that is no order in the normal sense, but only apophatically so.

While simple monotheism could perhaps justify monarchy, as Roman Catholic theologian Erik Peterson observed, the Trinitarian-egalitarian notion of God refuses all attempts at justifying this or that political order through a political theology. This, it could be added, is arguably why only a "negative political theology" is possible. The kingdom of God makes all political orders relative. It does not exist on the "same plane," so to speak, as the political order, which is why it doesn't simply compete or come into conflict with the political order. This does not mean, however, that the kingdom makes no difference in practice, but only that no particular practice or order should be confused for the kingdom.

8. See Athanasius, *De Sententia Dionysii* 22,2. Athanasius, *Orations against the Arians* 1,12. Cyril of Jerusalem, *Catechetical Lectures* 11,4. Gregory of Nazianzus, *Oration* 30,19. In the Creed of the Western Council of Serdica from 343, the kingly reign of the Son with the Father is said to be anarchos.

9. Gregory of Nazianzus, *On Human Nature* 1, 2; 14, 765.

10. Gregory of Nazianzus, *On the Holy Spirit* 1, 1; 3, 415. It can be discussed to which degree Gregory holds the "monarchian" view that God the Father is the "monarch" or whether he identified the divine monarchy with the Trinity as such, but both seem, paradoxically, to have been equally the case.

The kingdom is always paradoxically beyond all opposites and contradictions.

This should be insisted on when confronted by a number of attempts in contemporary theology to defend a hierarchical view of humanity. These are sometimes based on the notion that the Son of God is somehow subordinate to God the Father—and that this subordination should be reflected in human relations.[11] God the Father is eternally the one who commands, the argument goes, while Christ obeys. However, such "subordinationism" easily contradicts the classical doctrine of the Trinity, where it was only in his human nature that Christ could be said to submit himself to God. Christ, as God, is neither obedient nor disobedient, since these concepts only pertain to subordinates.[12] It could perhaps be argued that a kind of *egalitarian* complementarianism follows from the non-subordinationist notion of the Trinity, if by that we mean a view of persons as having complementary but equal functions. However, as for example Paul Fiddes has argued, there cannot even be said to be different "functions" in the Trinity but only different "appropriations" (Augustine) or expressions of the *same* function. Trinitarian theology cannot be made the model of a particular *order* among people, but only of the love that should permeate all human relations. The image of God is *equally* present in all human persons. This, however, is also why human nature is essentially incapable of definition, as Gregory of Nyssa argued. No human person can be reduced to this or that set of properties. Negative theology implies a negative anthropology that sees the infinite value of all humans as derived from God rather than whatever superficial properties we may have. Only a negative political theology is capable of taking this fully into account.

Isn't there a danger that if the idea of the kingdom as "anarchy" renders all political orders equally illegitimate, then we have no way of discerning between different political systems? If they're all equally "bad," then we can't distinguish between the most cruel

11. So-called "eternal functional subordination." This line of thought seems to be widespread in conservative evangelical theology.

12. Gregory of Nazianzus, *Oration* 30, 6.

dictatorships and peaceful liberal democracies, it seems. But while no political system should be confused with the kingdom of God, since the absolute difference remains, it could be argued that there may still be the possibility of an iconic or analogical similarity. If, however, similarity means participation, then surely it must also mean that the kingdom of God is actually present in some indirect way in any order that promotes freedom, love, and equality—even if participation should not be confused with identity. Only God is good, said Jesus (Mark 10:18), which for classical theology didn't mean that creation was evil, but only that the world is good to the degree that it participates *in* God. While all created reality is infinitely "distant" from God, as Gregory of Nyssa argued, its capacity to reflect God is restored to the degree that the fragments of the broken creation are healed and reconciled. There *is* a difference between war and peace, arrogance and humility, hatred and love.

It may also be argued that in a fallen world these high ideals (or what seems to be so) are impossible to maintain and that some degree of law and authority is necessary in order to avoid larger evils. This argument, made by Augustinian realism, is indeed very plausible and perhaps even unavoidable. This does not change the fact, however, that the kingdom of God consists in love and the freedom from all forms of domination and violence. It only makes it clearer, perhaps, that the kingdom of God is not of this world. This is why the kingdom, while not being an *ideal*, continues to challenge the church and society. In doing so, it also challenges our attempts at equating the kingdom with this or that political "-ism." Having initially used the notion of "Christian anarchism" for investigative purposes, I now suggest that we—in a good apophatic manner—leave also this concept behind in order to let the kingdom of God talk for itself.

Selective Bibliography

Agamben, Giorgio. "On Anarchy Today." https://illwill.com/on-anarchy-today.

———. *The Kingdom and the Glory: For a Theological Genealogy of Economy and Government.* Stanford, CA: Stanford University Press, 2011.

Barth, Karl. *Church Dogmatics, vol. II, 2.* Peabody, MA: Hendrickson, 2010.

———. *Church Dogmatics, vol. IV, 1.* Peabody, MA: Hendrickson, 2010.

———. *The Epistle to the Romans.* Oxford: Oxford University Press, 1933.

Bakunin, Mikhail. *God and the State.* New York: Dover, 1970.

Berdyaev, Nicolai. *Slavery and Freedom.* 2nd ed. San Rafael: Semantron, 2009.

Blumhardt, Christoph. *Action in Waiting.* Farmington, PA: Plough, 2014.

———. *The Gospel of God's Reign.* Walden, NY: Plough, 2019.

Brueggemann, Walter. *Sabbath as Resistance: Saying No to the Culture of Now.* Louisville: Westminster John Knox, 2017.

Cavanaugh, William T. "The City Beyond Secular Parodies." In *Radical Orthodoxy: A New Theology,* edited by John Milbank et al., 182–200. London: Routledge, 1998.

Campbell, Will D. *Crashing the Idols: The Vocation of Will D. Campbell.* Eugene, OR: Wipf & Stock, 2010.

Chelčický, Petr. *The Net of Faith—Book I: The Corruption of the Church, Caused by Its Fusion and Confusion with Temporal Power.* Translated by Enrico C. S. Molnár. 2006. https://archive.org/details/TheNetOfFaith/mode/2up

Chomsky, Noam. "The Kind of Anarchism I Believe in, and What's Wrong with Libertarians." Interview with Michael S. Wilson. *Alternet,* 2013. https://chomsky.info/20130528/.

Christoyannopoulos, Alexandre J. M. E. *Christian Anarchism: A Political Commentary on the Gospel.* Exeter: Imprint Academic, 2010.

Džalto, Davor. *Anarchy and the Kingdom of God: From Eschatology to Orthodox Political Theology and Back.* Orthodox Christianity and Contemporary Thought. New York: Fordham University Press, 2021.

Eller, Vernard. *Christian Anarchy: Jesus' Primacy over the Powers.* Grand Rapids: Eerdmans, 1987.

Ellul, Jacques. *Anarchy and Christianity.* Grand Rapids: Eerdmans, 1991.

———. *The Meaning of the City.* Grand Rapids: Eerdmans, 1970.

———. *The Subversion of Christianity.* Grand Rapids: Eerdmans, 1986.

Fiddes, Paul S. *Participating in God: A Pastoral Doctrine of the Trinity.* Louisville: Westminster John Knox, 2001.

Gregory of Nyssa. "On the 'Final Subjection' of Christ." In *On Death and Eternal Life,* translated by Brian Daley, 65–86. New York: Saint Vladimir's Seminary Press, 2022.

———. *St. Gregory of Nyssa: The Lord's Prayer, The Beatitudes.* Translated by Hilda C. Graef. New York: Paulist, 1978.

Gurney, John. *Gerrard Winstanley: The Digger's Life and Legacy.* Revolutionary Lives. London: Pluto, 2012.

Gushee, David P., and Stassen, Glen H. *Kingdom Ethics.* Downers Grove, IL: InterVarsity, 2003.

Hart, David Bentley. "Human Dignity Was a Rarity Before Christianity." *Church Life Journal,* 2017. https://churchlifejournal.nd.edu/articles/human-dignity-was-a-rarity-before-christianity/.

Kjær, Niels. *Kristendom og Anarkisme.* Brabrand: Self-published, 1972.

Köbner, Julius. *Manifest des Freien Urchristenthums an das deutsche Volk.* Hamburg: J.G. Oncken, 1848.

Moltmann, Jürgen. *The Crucified God.* Minneapolis: Fortress, 2015.

———. *The Power of the Powerless.* London: SCM, 1983.

Newheiser, David. "Why the World Needs Negative Political Theology." *Modern Theology* 36, 1 (2020) 5–12.

Origen, *Contra Celsum [Against Celsus].* Translated by Henry Chadwick. Cambridge: Cambridge University Press, 1980.

Peterson, Erik. *Theological Tractates.* Translated by Michael J. Hollerich. Stanford, CA: Stanford University Press, 2011.

Proudhon, Pierre-Joseph. *What is Property?* Cambridge: Cambridge University Press, 2020.

Rauschenbusch, Walter. *A Theology for The Social Gospel.* New York: Macmillan, 1917.

Sokolowski, Robert. *The God of Faith and Reason: Foundations of Christian Theology.* Washington, DC: Catholic University of America, 1995.

Steenbuch, Johannes Aakjær. *Guds rige er anarki: Evangeliet mellem magt og afmagt.* København: Fønix, 2019.

———. *Light of Light: How Trinitarian Theology Became a Thing, and Why It Matters.* Eugene: Cascade Books, 2026.

Steenwyk, Mark van. *That Holy Anarchist: Reflections on Christianity & Anarchism.* Minneapolis: Missio Dei, 2012.

Stringfellow, William. *An Ethic for Christians and Other Aliens in a Strange Land.* Eugene, OR: Wipf & Stock, 2004).

———. *A Keeper of the Word: Selected Writings of William Stringfellow.* Grand Rapids: Eerdmans, 1996.

Terpstra, M., and Wit, T. de. "'No Spiritual Investment in the World As It Is': Jacob Taubes's Negative Political Theology." In *Flight of the Gods:*

Philosophical Perspectives on Negative Theology, edited by Ilse N. Bulhof and Laurens ten Kate, 319–53. Kampen: Kok Agora, 2000.

Tolstoj, Lev. *On Anarchy.* Maldon: Free Age, 1900.

Weaver, J. Denny. *The Nonviolent Atonement.* Grand Rapids: Eerdmans, 2001.

Wink, Walter. *The Powers That Be: Theology for a New Millennium.* New York: Doubleday, 1998.

Wright, N. T. "The New Testament and the 'State.'" *Themelios* 16, 1 (1990) 11–17.

www.ingramcontent.com/pod-product-compliance
Lightning Source LLC
LaVergne TN
LVHW090535110826
845146LV00003B/1102

9798385243952